CREATING
THE CONDITIONS FOR
TEACHING
AND LEARNING

CREATING
THE CONDITIONS FOR
TEACHING
AND LEARNING

*A HANDBOOK OF STAFF
DEVELOPMENT ACTIVITIES*

**DAVID HOPKINS
and ALMA HARRIS**

with **COLETTE SINGLETON**
and **RUTH WATTS**

David Fulton Publishers
London

David Fulton Publishers Ltd
Ormond House, 26–27 Boswell Street, London WC1N 3JZ

www.fultonpublishers.co.uk

First published in Great Britain by David Fulton Publishers 2000

British Library Cataloguing in Publication Data
A catalogue record for this book is available from the British Library

ISBN 1–85346–689–1

The publishers would like to thank John Cox for copy-editing and Priscilla Sharland for proofreading this book.

Typeset by FiSH Books, London
Printed in Great Britain by Hobbs the Printers, Totton, Hants.

Contents

Acknowledgements   *vii*

Chapter 1 Creating the Conditions for Teaching and Learning   *1*

Chapter 2 Frameworks for Learning and Teaching   *5*

Chapter 3 Whole-Class Teaching   *13*
            – Activity 3.1: Use of Questioning   *22*

Chapter 4 Cooperative Group Work   *25*
            – Activity 4.1: Using Collaborative Teaching Techniques *31*

Chapter 5 Inductive Teaching   *35*
            – Activity 5.1: Inductive Teaching   *44*

Chapter 6 Synectics   *49*
            – Activity 6.1: Synectics   *54*

Chapter 7 Concept Attainment   *59*
            – Activity 7.1: Concept Attainment   *63*

Chapter 8 Assessment as a Tool for Learning   *67*
            – Activity 8.1: Formative Assessment and Learning   *71*

Chapter 9 The Staff Development Imperative   *77*

Chapter 10 Whole-School Strategies   *85*

References and Further Reading   *99*

Index   *101*

Acknowledgements

We are particularly grateful to colleagues at Swanwick Hall School, Derbyshire and Big Wood School, Nottingham for sharing the outcomes of their school improvement work with us and for allowing us to include them in this book. We are also grateful to: David Jackson, Pat Reynolds, Arianne Roberts and Clare Scammell for contributing to the fact in their different ways.

Dedication

This book is dedicated with affection and admiration to Bruce Joyce whose energy, commitment and wisdom has enhanced the classroom experience of generations of teachers and their students.

CHAPTER 1

Creating the Conditions for Teaching and Learning

School improvement is now a dominant theme in contemporary educational reform and development. The growing concern among politicians and the wider public about 'educational standards' has resulted in a variety of change interventions and initiatives. Some of these interventions have been government directed, while others have been initiated and developed locally. Yet, despite a wide range of activities in the name of improving student achievement, there is still a tendency to focus change efforts at the level of the school rather than the level of the classroom.

The approach to educational change which we call 'school improvement' has a different orientation. Our 'Improving the Quality of Education For All' (IQEA) school improvement project for example, focuses upon the teaching and learning process and the conditions that support it. It acknowledges that without an equal focus on the development capacity or internal conditions of the school, innovative work will soon become marginalised. The IQEA project works from an assumption that schools are most likely to strengthen their ability to provide enhanced outcomes for all students when they adopt ways of working that are consistent with both their own and the current reform agenda. Indeed, the schools we are currently working with are using the external drive to improve teaching and learning as a basis for conducting their own developmental work at the classroom level.

At the outset of IQEA we attempted to outline our vision of school improvement by articulating a set of principles that provided us with a philosophical and practical starting point (Ainscow *et al.* 1994). These principles represent the expectations we have of the way project schools pursue school improvement. They serve as an *aide-mémoire* to the schools and to ourselves. We feel that the operation of these principles creates synergism – together they are greater than the sum of their parts.

- School improvement is a process that focuses on enhancing the *quality of students' learning*.

1

- The vision of the school should be one which embraces *all* members of the school community as both learners and contributors.
- The school will secure its *internal priorities* through adopting external pressures for change and in so doing enhance its capacity for managing change.
- The school will seek to use data, action research and *enquiry* to drive forward and inform school improvement efforts.
- The school will seek to develop structures and create conditions that encourage collaboration and lead to the *empowerment* of students and teachers.

From our experience within the IQEA project we have identified a number of 'conditions' at school and classroom level that support and sustain school improvement. These conditions are the internal features of the school that enable the work to be completed (Ainscow *et al.* 1994, Hopkins *et al.* 1997). At school level, these conditions provide a working definition of the *development capacity* of the school. They represent the key management arrangements and can be broadly stated as:

- a commitment to *staff development*;
- practical efforts to *involve staff, students and the community* in school policies and decisions;
- *'transformational'* leadership approaches;
- *effective coordination* strategies;
- proper attention to the potential benefits of *enquiry and reflection*;
- a commitment to *collaborative planning activity*.

At the classroom level also, a set of conditions exist that facilitate and sustain effective teaching and learning. These classroom conditions are:

- *Authentic relationships* – the quality, openness and congruence of relationships existing in the classroom.
- *Rules and boundaries* – the pattern of expectations set by the teacher and school of student performance and behaviour within the classroom.
- *Planning, resources and preparation* – the access of teachers to a range of pertinent teaching materials and the ability to plan and differentiate these materials for a range of students.
- *Teacher's repertoire* – the range of teaching styles and models internalised and available to a teacher dependent on student, context, curriculum and desired outcome.
- *Pedagogic partnerships* – the ability of teachers to form professional relationships within and outside the classroom that focus on the study and improvement of practice.
- *Reflection on teaching* – the capacity of the individual teacher to reflect on his/her own practice, and to put to the test of practice, specifications of teaching from other sources.

Schools working within IQEA are encouraged to work upon the school level and classroom level conditions simultaneously. In our recent work, schools within the project have sought to integrate work at both levels by focusing upon different models of teaching in order to expand teachers' instructional repertoires. This focus has provided a basis for staff development and planning at the school level, as well as peer observation and innovation in the classroom. Having selected a particular model of teaching, each school places priority upon embedding the model into teachers' classroom practices. When this has been achieved, other models are added to further enhance the quality of teaching and learning within the school. This experience suggests that focusing upon models of teaching has enabled IQEA schools to build the capacity for change at both the school and classroom levels. It has also created a coherent programme of staff development within IQEA schools that impacts directly and positively upon student achievement and learning. It is this recent emphasis upon models of teaching that provides the focus for this book.

Who is the book for?

In writing this book we have in mind the teacher, or indeed groups of teachers, interested in classroom level change and development. In some cases such individuals may have responsibility for development work within the school. It may be a staff development coordinator or a curriculum deputy interested in improving the quality of teaching and learning within the school. It may be a subject leader or faculty head who has a clear view of effective teaching and wishes to extend this work with colleagues. Alternatively, it may be an individual teacher who wants to improve their own teaching. Whatever the motivation for reading this book, its intended outcome is to assist teachers in improving the quality of teaching and learning in the classroom.

What is the purpose of the book?

The purpose of this book is to provide some practical guidance for teachers in understanding and using the various models of teaching. We also use the words 'pedagogy' and 'instruction' to refer to the teaching process. The book is intended to offer an overview of those models that can be most easily incorporated into classroom practice within a wide range of subject areas. It also provides a series of practical illustrations of how each model can be used, and staff development activities to allow teachers to interrogate each model in greater depth. In summary, the book provides ideas and materials to help colleagues in schools to create the conditions for effective teaching and learning to take place.

What does the book do?

The book encourages teachers who are interested in developing their teaching to consider a wide range of different teaching models. To be effective within the classroom, teachers need to be constantly seeking to extend their teaching repertoire. This book provides suggestions, ideas and information that teachers can use to improve their practice. It also offers a coherent and strategic approach to staff development.

Where do the ideas come from?	The book is based on the work of Bruce Joyce and his colleagues, in particular *Models of Teaching* (Joyce and Weil 1996, 5th edn), and *Models of Learning – Tools for Teaching* (Joyce *et al*. 1997). It also draws upon the practical experience of the teachers involved in the IQEA project. The innovative ways in which they have applied different models of teaching within the classroom are represented in the illustrative figures, examples and the extension activities.
How should the book be used?	The book should be used as a guide and an introduction to the variety of 'models of teaching' (Joyce and Weil 1996). It offers a number of starting points for teachers interested in extending their teaching repertoire by incorporating new models. Some teachers will want to start with those models that have the most direct relevance and application to their subject teaching. Others will want to select models that require thought, imagination and tenacity to use within their subject area. A key task of those using the suggestions and materials will be to decide which model to trial and for what purpose.

This book is essentially about improving the quality of teaching and learning. It is a practical handbook and not a theoretical text. It has been written for teachers in an attempt to secure change at the classroom level, where it matters most. We hope that it will encourage teachers to embark upon classroom innovation that will contribute to improved learning outcomes for all their students.

In this book we also present a view of teaching that is somewhat at odds with the current emphasis on target setting that puts pressure on schools and teachers to raise levels of achievement in the short term. To summarise our position briefly, effective teaching reflects the teacher's ability to create powerful learning experiences for students. Successful teachers are not as Joyce and Showers note, 'simply charismatic, persuasive, and expert presenters; rather, they provide their students with powerful cognitive and social tasks and teach them how to make productive use of them' (Joyce and Showers 1991, p. 10). The important point is that powerful learning, at least in schools, does not occur by accident. It is usually the result of an effective learning situation created by a skillful teacher. As Bruce Joyce and Beverly Showers (1991, p. 12) say:

> Effective teachers are confident that they can make a difference and that the difference is made by increasing their own teaching repertoires and the learning repertoires of their students. Put simply, powerful teachers believe that all children can learn and that they can teach all children. More pertinently, they convey this message to their students.

CHAPTER 2

Frameworks for Learning and Teaching

Introduction

Despite the contemporary emphasis on the importance of classroom practice, the language of discourse about teaching by teachers in England remains in general at a restricted level. Teachers in other European countries and North America for example, appear to use a far more elaborate language in which to talk about teaching and have more sophisticated frameworks against which to reflect on their practice. Even in those instances where more precision of language is achieved, there also needs to be operational definitions against which teachers can assess their own practice and thereby develop and expand their range of classroom practices.

Quality teaching and learning needs to be underpinned by more elaborate and explicit frameworks for learning and teaching. This is particularly important as the research evidence on teaching and curriculum and its impact on student learning demonstrates that:

- There are a number of well-developed models of teaching and curriculum that generate substantially higher levels of student learning than does normative practice.
- The most effective curricular and teaching patterns induce students to construct knowledge – to inquire into subject areas intensively. The result is to increase student capacity to learn and work smarter.
- The most effective models of curriculum and teaching increase learning capacity for all students, greatly reducing the effects of gender, socio-economic status, linguistic background, and learning styles as factors in student learning.

Each of these conclusions emphasises the importance of the link between effective teaching and effective learning. The purpose of teaching is not only to help students to acquire curriculum knowledge but also to assist them in becoming powerful learners. Effective teachers find ways of raising levels of attainment while at the same time helping students become more powerful learners by expanding and making articulate their repertoire of learning strategies. Powerful learning refers to the ability of learners to respond successfully to the tasks that they are set, as well as the tasks they set themselves – in particular to:

- integrate prior and new knowledge;
- acquire and use a range of learning skills;
- solve problems individually and in groups;
- think carefully about their successes and failures;
- evaluate conflicting evidence and to think critically;
- accept that learning involves uncertainty and difficulty.

The deployment of such a range of learning strategies is commonly termed *meta-cognition*, which can be regarded as the learner's ability to take control over their own learning processes. The central characteristic of effective teachers is their ability to create powerful learners as well as knowledgeable students. The purpose of the framework for teaching proposed below, is to help all teachers to do just that.

A framework for teaching and learning

Our framework for teaching revolves around the following three aspects of teaching:

- teaching behaviours and skills
- teaching relationships
- teaching models.

These are three distinctive but not mutually exclusive ways of considering effective teaching.

Teaching behaviours and skills

There is an extensive research literature on teaching skills. Consistently high correlations are achieved between student achievement scores and the teacher's classroom behaviour (see Brophy and Good 1986, Creemers 1994). One general conclusion stands out: 'The most consistently replicated findings link achievement to the quantity and pacing of instruction' (Brophy and Good, p. 360). The amount learned is as Good (1989) subsequently noted, determined in part by opportunity to learn, which is determined by four broad teacher behaviours:

- First, effective teachers are businesslike and task-oriented. They emphasise instruction as basic to their role, expect students to master the curriculum, and allocate most classroom time to those activities that have relevant academic objectives.
- Second, effective teachers frequently use classroom organisation and management strategies that maximise the time students spend engaged in academic activities.

- Third, effective teachers allow students to move through the curriculum briskly but also successfully.
- Fourth, effective teachers spend most of their time actively instructing their students in group lessons or supervising their work on assignments rather than allowing students to spend inordinate time on individual seatwork practice without supervision or feedback.

Classroom studies of teaching effects have generally supported a direct and structured approach to instruction. Students usually achieve more when a teacher:

- Emphasises academic goals, makes them explicit, and expects students to be able to master the curriculum.
- Carefully organises and sequences curriculum experiences.
- Clearly explains and illustrates what students are to learn.
- Frequently asks direct and specific questions to monitor students' progress and check their understanding.
- Provides students with ample opportunity to practise, gives prompts and feedback to ensure success, corrects mistakes, and allows students to use a skill until it is over-learned or automatic.
- Reviews regularly and holds students accountable for work.

(Doyle 1987, p. 96)

From this perspective, a teacher promotes student learning by being active in planning and organising his or her teaching, explaining to students what they are to learn, arranging occasions for guided practice, monitoring progress, providing feedback and generally helping students understand and accomplish work.

At the heart of the teacher's work, of course, is classroom management. If classrooms are to be places where students can feel safe to concentrate on the learning, teachers have to be skilled in organising and managing large groups of people within a relatively confined space. Evertson and Harris (1992, p. 76) for example, have identified the following highlights of research on classroom management:

- Use time as effectively as possible.
- Implement group strategies with high levels of involvement and low levels of misbehaviour.
- Choose lesson formats and academic tasks conducive to high student engagement.
- Communicate clearly rules of participation.
- Prevent problems by implementing a system at the beginning of the school year.

Within our school improvement work we use short summaries of research evidence to stimulate discussion between groups of colleagues. For example, Kounin (1970), in his classic study, identified several strategies that teachers use to elicit high levels of work involvement and low levels of misbehaviour:

- *Withitness* – communicating awareness of student behaviour.
- *Overlapping* – doing more than one thing at once.
- *Smoothness and momentum* – moving in and out of activities smoothly with appropriately paced and sequenced instruction; and
- *Group alerting* – keeping all students attentive to a whole-group focus.

Other useful sources concerning teaching behaviours or skills include Good and Brophy (1987), Kyriacou (1986, 1991) and some of the other studies highlighted earlier in this chapter.

Teaching relationships

There are another set of factors that characterise effective teaching. These are less technical and are more related to the teacher's 'artistry'. Artistry incorporates the recognition that teaching involves creativity and is carried out in a highly personalised way. While this need not deny the potential value of considering particular models of teaching or examining the impact of specific skills, it draws attention to the fact that once in the classroom each teacher has the sole responsibility for creating the conditions within which each student can learn effectively. This must involve a degree of previous planning but it also requires a capacity to improvise and respond to classroom challenges in a creative way. Even the best-defined lesson plan has to be adapted to take account of unforeseen happenings. Indeed the artistry of a very successful teacher involves this ability to engage with, and turn to advantage, events and responses that could not have been anticipated.

This aspect of teaching, sometimes called the artistry of teaching, is well summed up by Lou Rubin (1985, p. v) when he comments:

> There is a striking quality to fine classrooms. Students are caught up in learning; excitement abounds; and playfulness and seriousness blend easily because the purposes are clear, the goals sensible, and an unmistakable feeling of well being prevails. Artist teachers achieve these qualities by knowing both their subject matter and their students; by guiding the learning with deft control – a control that itself is born out of perceptions, intuition, and creative impulse.

It is much more difficult to report research evidence that arises from this frame of reference. The evidence does not lend itself readily to specifications or lists of features. Yet this perspective on teachers' work is one that is immediately recognised by practitioners and, indeed, others in the wider community. It is not uncommon for teachers to be told by friends from outside the profession of the 'teacher who made a difference'. The personality, flair and emotional intelligence of the individual teacher is increasingly receiving belated attention (Hargreaves 2000).

Teaching models

Despite the impressive gains associated in the research literature with the range of teaching skills described earlier, they should be regarded as a necessary but not sufficient condition for effective teaching. There is an equally strong body of research and practice that suggests that student achievement can be further enhanced by the consistent and strategic use of specific teaching models (Joyce and Weil 1996, Joyce *et al.* 1997). As is seen in the following chapters, there are many powerful models of teaching – each with their own 'syntax', phases and guidelines – that are designed to bring about particular kinds of learning and to help students become more effective learners.

As was implied earlier, models of teaching are really models of learning. As students acquire information, ideas, skills, values, ways of thinking, and means of expressing themselves, they are also learning how to learn. In fact, the most important long-term outcome of instruction may be the students' increased capabilities to learn more easily and effectively in the future both because of the knowledge and skill they have acquired, and because they have mastered learning processes. How teaching is conducted has a large impact on students' abilities to educate themselves.

It is important to be clear about what is meant by a 'model of teaching'. One can regard the research on teaching effects or teaching skills as providing the teacher with, say, tactical knowledge. The research on 'models of teaching' on the other hand gives teachers more strategic knowledge about how to create whole-classroom settings to facilitate learning.

A well known, if dated example, of a model of teaching is that of the Humanities Curriculum Project (HCP). This curriculum was developed under the aegis of the Schools Council in England by a team led by Lawrence Stenhouse (1975). Within this curriculum, discussion was the main mode of inquiry and the teacher acted as a neutral chairperson. Discussion was informed and disciplined by evidence, such as items from history, journalism and literature. This particular curriculum approach inevitably placed new kinds of demand on both teachers and students (Rudduck 1984, p. 57). For example:

New skills for most teachers:
- Discussion rather than instruction.
- Teacher as neutral chairperson.
- Teacher talk reduced to about 15 per cent of the total talking done in the classroom.
- Teacher handling material from different disciplines.
- New modes of assessment.

New skills for most students:
- Discussion, not argument or debate.
- Listening to, and talking to, each other, not just the teacher.
- Taking initiatives in contributing – not being cued by the teacher.

There is a danger that centrally designed curricula can become blueprints that inhibit autonomy in teaching and learning. In that respect it is interesting to note that the Humanities Curriculum as a model of teaching is specific rather than prescriptive. Although it defined the educational encounter, it also encouraged teachers to experiment with the specificity rather than be bound by the prescription. From this perspective, the process model of curriculum, as described by Stenhouse (1975), is liberating or emancipatory because it encourages independence of thought and argument on the part of the student, and experimentation and the use of judgement on the part of the teacher. When teachers adopt this experimental approach to their teaching they are taking on an educational idea, cast in the form of a curriculum proposal and testing it out within their classrooms. It is in this way that the use of 'teaching models' form part of an overall strategy for school improvement.

In *Models of Learning – Tools for Teaching* (Joyce *et al.* 1997), a range of contrasting and complementary teaching strategies are described. In this book we describe the structure or syntax of the different models. This refers to the major elements and phases, how they are put together and their main instructional and nurturant effects. All of the models that we use and describe are research based in so far as they have been developed and refined through cycles of research and development and have proven effectiveness. There is always a series of core principles that underpin each model that hold true in the various manifestations a model may take. When these models and strategies are combined, they have even greater potential for improving student learning.

In the following chapters we give examples of models of teaching and learning for:

- extracting information and ideas from lectures and presentations (Chapter 3);
- working effectively with others to initiate and carry out cooperative tasks (Chapter 4);
- building hypotheses and theories (Chapter 5);
- using metaphors to think creatively (Chapter 6);
- memorising information (Chapter 7);
- attaining concepts and how to invent them (Chapter 7).

Despite the emphasis on teaching in this book, we do not underestimate the contribution of assessment to both teaching and learning. In Chapter 8 we emphasise the importance of feedback, the explicit use of criteria, and the role of formative assessment in effective teaching. We also recognise that powerful teaching and learning occurs in powerful schools. As Lawrence Downey (1967) once put it: 'A school teaches in three ways, by what it teaches, by how it teaches and by the kind of place it is.' In the final two chapters of the book we describe and give examples of the school contexts and conditions that support effective teaching and learning.

Now imagine a classroom where the learning environment contains a variety of models of teaching that are not only intended to accomplish a range of curriculum goals, but are also designed to help students increase their competence as learners. In such classrooms the students learn models for memorising information, how to attain concepts and how to invent them. They practise building hypotheses and theories and using the tools of science to test them. They learn how to extract information and ideas from lectures and presentations, how to study social issues and how to analyse their own social values. These students also know how to profit from training and how to train themselves in athletics, performing arts, mathematics and social skills. They know how to make their writing and problem-solving more lucid and creative. Perhaps most importantly, they know how to take initiative in planning personal study, and they know how to work with others to initiate and carry out cooperative tasks. As students succeed in mastering information and skills, the result of each learning experience is not only the content they learn but also the greater ability they acquire to approach future learning tasks effectively and to create better learning environments for themselves.

We believe that the evidence from research on teaching can help teachers create effective learning environments for the students. However, such research and strategies should not be regarded as prescriptive. Research knowledge and the various specifications of teaching can prove limited, especially if they are adopted uncritically. Such knowledge only becomes useful when it is subjected to the discipline of practice through the exercise of the teacher's professional judgement. For, as Lawrence Stenhouse (1975, p. 142) said, such proposals are not to be regarded 'as an unqualified recommendation, but rather as a provisional specification claiming no more than to be worth putting to the test of practice. Such proposals claim to be intelligent rather than correct.'

As we emphasise throughout this book, outstanding teachers take individual and collective responsibility to base their teaching on the best knowledge and practice available. They then take those ideas and reflect upon them through practice in their own and each other's classrooms.

CHAPTER 3

Whole-Class Teaching

In active whole-class teaching the teacher orchestrates students' learning and seeks to improve performance through direct instruction, whole-class questioning, discussion and learning activities.

Vignette

A class of Year 7 students is being introduced to rhythm in poetry, as part of a unit on sound effects in language. The objectives of the lesson are to refine students' listening powers, in particular their sense of volume, beat and pace; to appreciate the force of repetition and variation of tempo; to understand the relationship between meaning and beat; to appreciate how writers use these elements to create dramatic effects in their writing. The teacher has chosen Vachel Lindsay's ballad, *The Daniel Jazz*, as an example.

The lesson begins with the title of the poem. The class are asked to work out what it means. Who was Daniel? What has jazz got to do with him? There is a whole-class discussion to ascertain prior knowledge, using a range of questioning techniques. Taking the medley of ideas, the teacher builds up a complete version of the story for the class.

The teacher then develops the jazz/story connection and challenges the class to say what they undestand by 'jazz writing'. Students are asked to write down at least two ideas on the relationship between music and words. Students share their ideas with the person next to them and together they attempt to produce two or three more ideas.

After a few minutes the teacher asks for responses to the questions and elicits terms which might include: DRUM BEAT, RHYTHM, NOISE, LOUD, FAST, SLOW, BASS, TIMING, REPETITION, etc. Some of these concepts are written on the board and stay as reference points for the rest of the lesson.

The teacher then displays the first ten lines of *The Daniel Jazz*. The teacher reads the first four lines and asks if any of the words on the board apply to this section of the poem. The class recites the lines together, emphasising the beat. A *Sun* newspaper report of the Daniel incident at a local zoo is introduced to the class. The class try to recite it but fail. The difference between the two pieces of writing is posed as a question to the class.

In pairs, the class are asked to identify any differences in pace and rhythm in the first 20 lines of the poem. After a few minutes the pairs report back with examples.

Follow-up work includes:

- Rehearsal and performance of the whole poem with choral and solo parts, sound effects and rhythmic accompaniments.

- Writing a class ballad using *The Daniel Jazz* as a template example.

- More advanced work on word and sound, syllabic effects, repetitions and variations in tempo.

Description of the Whole-Class Teaching Model

This model of teaching enables students to order, absorb, understand and relate different areas of knowledge efficiently. It is not a matter of instruction alone. As well as enabling students to process information, the model also allows for student interaction so that they learn from each other as well as the teacher and extend their repertoire of social skills. Whole-class teaching is about talking with students, listening to them and guiding their learning activities.

Whole-class active teaching is essentially composed of three major components:

- Students are formally presented with a problem, issue, area of knowledge, set of skills through lecture or demonstration.
- Students develop understanding through systematic questioning and disciplined enquiry.
- Students apply understanding through a series of set tasks.

The model presupposes a coherent instructional programme based on a clear set of overarching goals. The model though is not inclusive to these goals. The instructional model works as part of an integrative teaching and learning plan that may include cooperative group work and independent study. Employing a range of teaching activities influences student motivation and is likely to engage them in learning. Non-stop teacher presentation or instruction involving taking notes, answering questions from textbooks and recycling information in homework is tedious and repetitive. Mixing the palette of teaching approaches is more likely to engage students in learning, as will mixing modes of delivery and format.

As implied in the previous chapter, there is a significant amount of research evidence confirming certain teacher behaviours as being consistent with high quality learning. Within a whole-class teaching context these have been seen to be (Creemers 1994):

- *Management of the classroom* to create a situation where learning can take place. This implies an orderly and quiet atmosphere in the classroom, although learning itself requires more than a well organised class. Moreover, effective teaching itself contributes to the management of the class.

- *Provision of homework.* If properly organised, homework contributes to effectiveness. This implies a clear structure of assignments, and supervision and evaluation of homework.

- *Expectations* that teachers (and schools) have of their abilities to influence student outcomes probably influence what teachers do. We can expect those expectations to become apparent in actual teacher behaviours.

- *Clear goal-setting.* This includes a restructured set of goals, and an emphasis on basic skills and on cognitive learning and transfer. The content should be chosen in line with these goals.

- *Structuring the content.* This includes the ordering of the content according to the hierarchically ordered goals. The use of advance organisers can also structure the content for students. The use of prior knowledge can increase students' own contributions and responsiveness for learning.

- *Clarity of presentation*, which implies the elements mentioned above but also refers to the transfer process itself (avoiding vagueness and incomplete sentences).

- *Questioning* (by means of low and higher order questions) keeps students at work and can be used to check their understanding.

- *Evaluating* whether the goals are obtained, by means of testing, providing feedback and corrective instruction.

It is important to emphasise that whole-class teaching is a strategic approach to teaching that not only focuses on basic skills and cognitive processes, but also on promoting learning strategies, problem-solving and social support. Teachers using the whole-class model address these more complex instructional goals by using a range of techniques to structure strategic learning. Some of these key strategies are:

Understanding. This is a prerequisite to clarity and involves matching the new information to the learners' present knowledge. Does the teacher

    a. Determine students' existing familiarity with the information presented?

    b. Use terms that are unambiguous and within the students' experience?

Structuring. This involves organising the material to promote a clear presentation; stating the purpose, reviewing main ideas, and providing transitions between sections. Does the teacher

    a. Establish the purpose of the lesson?

    b. Preview the organisation of the lesson?

    c. Include internal summaries of the lesson?

Sequencing. This involves arranging the information in an order conducive to learning, typically by gradually increasing its difficulty of complexity. Does the teacher order the lesson in a logical way, appropriate to the content and the learners?

Explaining. When explaining principles and relating them to facts through examples, illustrations or analogies, does the teacher

    a. Define major concepts?

    b. Give examples to illustrate these concepts?

    c. Use examples that are accurate and concrete as well as abstract?

Presenting. This refers to volume, pacing, articulation, and other speech mechanics. Does the teacher

    a. Articulate words clearly and project speech loudly enough?

    b. Pace the sections of the presentation at rates conducive to understanding?

    c. Support the verbal content with appropriate non-verbal communication and visual aids?

(Good and Brophy 1984)

As well as clarity of objectives and appropriateness of methods, the successful implementation of whole-class teaching needs to consider the classroom management context. Rules help manage students' learning behaviour. Discussion, whether whole-class or group, is most effective where clear ground rules apply. Rules discipline discussion, offer security to the less confident, curb the dominant, bring out the self-effacing. Typically such rules for whole-class discussion establish the teacher as chairperson, insist on respect for all contributions and agree that these are spread evenly across the class by use of techniques such as 'numbered heads' or 'snowballing' described in the next chapter.

Sequencing of activities in whole-class teaching is crucial to its success. An inexperienced, unruly, or fractious class, may have to be guided towards disciplined debate. Thus the teacher may decide to commence discussion with a simple sequence of questions before moving to the more demanding orchestration of all-class discussion.

*Syntax of the
Whole-Class
Teaching Model*

The whole-class model of teaching includes the following five phases.

Phase One: Review

- Review the concepts and skills from the previous lesson (and, if appropriate, the homework).

Phase Two: Presenting information

Lecture or talk:

- Preview the outline and scope of the lecture.
- Introduce key terms or concepts.
- Lecture proceeds in small steps, starting with what is familiar and using lively explanations and illustrations.

Demonstration:

- Preliminaries – a guide as to what to observe and expect.
- Preview – purpose is outlined.
- Rehearsal – teachers go through each step.
- Reprise – procedures are repeated.

Phase Three: Involving students in discussion

- Focus on meaning and promoting student understanding through fast-paced discussion.
- Assess student comprehension through high quality questioning.

Phase Four: Engaging students in learning activities

- Design activities to focus on content.
- Implementation of learning activities.

Phase Five: Summary and review

- Students ask follow-up questions, share findings and conclusions.
- Teacher reinforces key points, emphasises central ideas and sums up achievements.

*Elaboration of
the Whole-Class
Teaching Model*

There are **three** main components of this teaching model:

1. Presenting information.
2. Involving students in discussion.
3. Engaging students in discrete tasks and learning activities.

1. Presenting information

The two pivotal teacher-directed modes of conveying information are:

- lecture/talk;
- demonstration.

The lecture/talk

This is a justified strategy where:

- information is not readily available to students;
- where as a digest it saves classroom time;
- where it guides subsequent thinking and approaches by setting an agenda;
- where it is part of a learning polemic aiming to provoke and challenge students;
- where diffuse ideas need to be synthesised, after discussion for example;
- where a new topic needs to be introduced.

One of the main drawbacks of the lecture is that it can render students passive. Dynamic delivery, interspersing new ideas with graphic presentation, can make the lecture a highly effective mode of conveying information and generating student interest.

The most effective lectures include the following three features:

1. The topic is trailed by a preview of the outline and scope of the lecture.
2. Key terms or concepts are introduced to the class and displayed prominently.
3. The body of the lecture proceeds in small steps, starting with what is familiar to students before leading then into unfamiliar territory.

Testing student understanding through questioning is an important element of effective lecturing. So are other forms of student engagement like taking votes, sampling opinion through simple questionnaires, alternating talk with demonstration, mixing exposition with performance, allowing time for recollection and recapping. Finally, effective lecturers review progress and point the way forward. They lead into the next activity and direct its content and or purpose.

Effective lectures are also precise. A direct and simple style characterised by concrete illustrations, apt analogies and well-defined technical terms delivered with enthusiasm and conviction encourages concentration and develops student understanding.

Demonstration

The second mode of information presentation is demonstration. The demonstration process is divided into four main steps:

1. *Preliminaries.* A description of equipment, instruments, appliances, and their safe use, a guide as to what to observe and expect and a general raising of expectation.
2. *Preview.* The purpose of the demonstration is outlined, the audience prepared and focused on the object of the lesson, e.g. a lab experiment on respiration, a demonstration on how to use a lathe, a performance of mime techniques.
3. *Rehearsal.* Teachers go through each step, announcing intentions, commenting on what they are doing, verbalising their actions, using and reusing technical terms (words can be printed on card, laminated, cut up and then displayed using velcro down the side of the black–whiteboard).
4. *Reprise.* Procedures are repeated to habituate students to the practices and expertise of the subject.

To monitor student comprehension, effective demonstrations include questioning or students are asked to repeat demonstrations themselves. This offers opportunities for the teacher to give corrective feedback. In order to maintain a high level of student concentration and interest, teachers may stop the process and ask the class to suggest what might come next, or to comment at the end of the lesson on the success of the demonstration.

2. Involving students in discussions

Discourse in the classroom covers a range of student–teacher exchange from fast-paced review through to thoughtful discussion. Review tests and reinforces previous learning, centres on recall and is conducted at a brisk pace. Recitation is concerned less with eliciting 'right answers' and more to do with reflection and commentary. So, an English teacher, recapping on literary terms introduced in an earlier lesson, might start a new session by quizzing a class about metaphor, simile, personification and ask them to identify them in some sample sentences displayed for the purpose. The next stage of the lesson might include a question/answer session on a poem, in which the teacher asks students to identify figurative language (review) and then to explain what the effects of the figures are (recitation). This tutor-directed exchange might then be steered into more open ground and concentrate on meaning, where there are no 'right answers' and opinion has to be evidenced and articulated (discussion).

The effectiveness of any teacher–student exchange depends on the nature of the questioning. The quality of the questions asked and especially their sequencing are the two critical features of the discussion process. Whether questions elicit knowledge or comprehension, the crucial point is that they must be related to teaching goals. Any series of questions should be a mix of types and promote higher order thinking.

Poor quality questioning involves questions that predetermine answers. The rhetorical question suggests that the questioner doesn't really want an answer. Similarly, 'yes'/'no' questions may be useful as lesson warm-ups but they fail to involve the student and encourage thoughtless guessing.

In contrast good questions are:

- clear
- purposeful
- brief
- natural
- thought-provoking
- sequenced.

It is this latter feature that particularly determines the effectiveness of teacher–student exchanges. Low-level factual questions begin the sequence and provide the basis for the next set of questions which might be designed to encourage hypothesising, and speculation and analysis.

The manner in which questions are put to students and the way responses are handled also determines the effectiveness of teacher–student exchange. Rhetorical questions, as described above, suggest to the students that any response is redundant and not valued. So too, the 'nagging' question suggests teacher impatience and maybe read as coercion to which students' responses are negative, either self-defensive or submissive. A well-handled discussion session mixes factual with thought-provoking questions and allows time for responses. In addition, pacing, and wait-time that allows students to process answers are important factors in developing successful classroom exchanges. Rephrasing questions, offering subordinate ones or helpful clues, and acknowledging good answers, are ways successful teachers nurture genuine responses. Creating a 'benevolent' and supportive context for discussion is a prerequisite for effective classroom exchange.

3. Engaging students in discrete tasks and learning activities

This is the third element of teacher-directed learning and allows students time to practice and apply what they have learnt. There are two major aspects of these activities:

- design
- implementation.

Design

Well-designed activities are those that, first, relate to the goals of the unit being taught and focus upon students' understanding of content. In designing activities teachers may well apply the criterion of relevance, distinguishing between work that is essential, relevant and marginal to declared goals. It may be that some planned activities meet immediate if not long-term goals, and teachers select work on the basis of secondary criteria. For instance, a new programme might begin with activities designed solely to improve motivation, to engage and enthuse. Subsequently, goal-directed activities will be introduced.

A well-designed activity will not only be appropriate to overall learning goals but will be feasible. The benefits to students will outweigh costs in terms of time and effort. Benefit should be measured in terms of significant learning gains such as opportunities to work cooperatively and creatively, to engage with ideas, reflect critically and discuss thoughtfully.

Implementation

The second essential feature of effective learning activities is implementation. There are four stages in this process:

1. Teachers need to explain to students the purpose of planned activities so that they have a clear sense of direction in their work. Teachers need to contextualise the programme by explaining how it fits in with previous projects, what information will be required for success and how tasks might be completed.

2. Teachers need to structure students' learning approaches by offering guidance on reading, pointers to critical terminology, self-help revision guides or examples, helpful questions, guidance on note-taking, recording data, etc. Teachers who explain carefully and demonstrate with examples either at the start of a lesson or at critical junctures during the lesson are more likely to create effective learning environments.

3. Student progress should be monitored. Teachers should move round the class, helping where necessary, prompting rather than policing. This light surveillance will reveal how well students are managing tasks set and tell the teacher whether more whole-class instruction is needed.

4. Student feedback. Time needs to be provided for class and teacher to reflect upon progress, for students to ask follow-up questions, share findings and conclusions, and for the teacher to reinforce points, emphasise central ideas and sum up achievements.

Activity 3.1: Use of Questioning

Aim

- To improve classroom questioning techniques by analysing existing practice through collaborative activity.

This activity comprises two parts.

Part 1 – Step 1   As a department or within subject areas identify some recent lessons that were felt to be effective. Compile a list of the typical questions asked. How far does this list reflect the purposes below?

Purpose of questions

- To check extent of prior learning.
- To check and stimulate recall.
- To stimulate interest, involvement and depth of thinking.
- To identify future learning needs.
- To review and consolidate main points of the lesson.
- To diagnose learning difficulties.
- To create stimulating start to lesson.
- To draw on the ideas of some students for benefit of others.
- To encourage the expression of opinion and feelings.
- To stimulate language development and reasoning skills.

Step 2   How far were the questions asked open or closed?

Were *open* questions asked in order to:
- Provide greater opportunities for students to demonstrate their new knowledge?
- Diagnose lack of understanding and learning problems?
- Stimulate higher order thinking?
- Encourage language development?
- Encourage the expression of feelings and emotions?

Were *closed* questions asked in order to:
- Enable prior knowledge to be assessed?
- Test precise recall?
- Aid rapid repetition of key facts and thus help memorisation?

In pairs, plan a lesson where 'open' questions predominate.

Step 3   Share this with the group.

Part 2 – Step 1   A demonstration lesson is viewed on video and significant features of the questioning strategies used are noted and recorded individually.

Step 2   In pairs, teachers exchange their notes and views about the lesson.

Step 3   Each pair is asked to focus on *one* of the following features of questioning strategy.

---

1. *The spread.* Are all students given a chance to answer, or a few favoured ones? Are boys more favoured than girls? How are questions distributed?
2. *Tone.* Is the teacher enthusiastic or inquisitorial? Sympathetic and patient, or authoritarian and peremptory?
3. *Prompts.* Does the teacher nudge and guide hesitant students with sub-questions or helpful rephrasing or encouragement in various forms? Is the teacher a critical listener/prompter or does the teacher accept any answer irrespective of whether it is right or wrong? How does the teacher deal with inadequate answers? Offers a second, third chance?
4. *Wait-time.* Does the teacher tolerate thought-time and wait for answers. Does the teacher allow a number of attempts at answers? Does the teacher allow jotting-down-time for framing responses?
5. *Consolidation.* Does the teacher allow breathing spaces for reviewing progress, for trying again.
6. *Body language.* Facial expression, eye contact, tone of voice (see above), pose, mobility, gestures. Does the teacher use a wide, medium, narrow range of gestural communication?
7. *Pace.* Slow questioning can be dramatic especially if delivered with lowered voice and emphatic gestures. Dramatic pausing can give life to questions. And accelerating the pace of questioning can raise the tempo, energy and motivation of the class. Does the teacher use simple theatrical or performance techniques?
8. *Surveillance.* To what extent does the teacher monitor attention and responsiveness or use questions to check on levels of engagement in the class.

Step 4   The video is played again and notes are taken on the specific element identified.

Step 5   These views are shared initially in pairs and then as a whole group.

Step 6   Guidelines for effective questioning are drawn up within the department/ subject area.

CHAPTER 4

Cooperative Group Work

Cooperative group work is a model of teaching where students, working together in small groups on a range of academic problems can develop both their social and intellectual skills.

> **Vignette**
>
> A Religious Education class have been studying the beginnings of Christianity and its development within the Roman Empire. The teacher wants students to explore the notion of religious toleration and to begin to understand some of the political and cultural factors that define and determine the relationships between different religions.
>
> At the beginning of the lesson students are divided into nine named teams of four. Each student is given a number between 1 and 4 and is told that when their number and team name is called out, they have to stand up and answer whatever question has been asked.
>
> Once this 'numbered heads' strategy has been explained and the group composition determined, each student is asked to write down what they can remember of the last lesson on the spread of Christianity in the Eastern Mediterranean. This is shared with the group. After a few minutes the teacher calls out team names and numbers. Individual students are asked to summarise their previous learning. If satisfied with the answers given, the teacher then writes on the board, 'How tolerant were the Romans of other religions?' and explains that this is the question the class, working in groups, is going to explore in the lesson. There follows a brief introduction from the teacher using a map display to show the major concentrations and spread of three religious groups – Jews, Christians, Druids – across the Empire.

The class then divide into groups for 20 minutes. Three groups are to research Christians, three the Jews, and three the Druids. Each group is given a list of resources and a set of basic questions to answer. Each group must find out about four aspects (topics) of their allocated religion and their adherents:

1. beliefs
2. practices
3. location
4. how they were regarded and treated by the Romans.

Each group becomes expert in the various research areas.

Following the allocated time, and using the 'jigsaw' design, the 'expert' groups are dispersed into mixed groups of four. Each group then makes a presentation outlining its main findings and conclusion to the rest of the class.

Description of the Cooperative Group Work Teaching Model

As a model of teaching cooperative group work has a powerful effect in raising student achievement because it harnesses the synergy of collective action. It combines the dynamics of democratic processes with the processes of academic enquiry. It encourages active participation in learning and collaborative behaviour by developing social as well as 'academic' skills. Thus the model requires students to practise and refine their negotiating, organising and communication skills, define issues and problems and develop ways of solving them including collecting and interpreting evidence, hypothesising, testing and re-evaluating.

The model is highly flexible and draws on a wide range of methods – individual research, collaborative enquiry and plenary activities – and allows the integration of them all into a powerful teaching tool. The teacher is able to conduct a more subtle and complex learning strategy that achieves a number of learning goals simultaneously. Thus, styles can vary from didactic to 'light touch' teaching where the teacher is more an adviser and guide than a director.

Examples of cooperative learning strategies

As illustrated in the vignette, 'numbered heads' and 'jigsawing' were used and are very popular approaches to cooperative group learning. Below are two further examples of these approaches.

Numbered heads

In an English lesson the teacher is focusing on the punctuation of direct and indirect speech. First, the class is divided into named groups of four and each student is allocated a number. From a displayed passage of unpunctuated dialogue and description each group is asked to identify the direct speech. Everyone knows that after two minutes of discussion there will be silence signalled by a bell ringing and that one of them will have their number called and will have to respond. This motivates groups to share information and make sure everyone knows the answer. It gives every student a chance to shine and, because they have group support, no one is made anxious about answering. Successful responses bolster both individual and collective confidence that can be boosted further by some form of team award system.

Jigsaw

In Food Technology a teacher sets up a question or problem for enquiry and divides students into equal-sized groups called Home Groups. Typical topics might include food hygiene in the home, safe practice in the kitchen, processed versus organic foodstuffs, dangerous additives and so on. Each group is given an identical task and suggested list of roles/jobs. For five minutes groups discuss the 'problem' and allocate roles/jobs. The Home Groups then divide and those with identical jobs form new Expert Groups whose function is to collect relevant information. After a period of research the original Home Groups are reformed and expert knowledge pooled to solve the problem or map the issue.

The following are further examples of cooperative learning strategies (Hopkins *et al.* 1994).

Twos to fours or snowballing

Children work together in pairs, perhaps upon a mathematical problem or science experiment. They then join with another pair to explain what they have achieved, and to compare this with the work of the other pair. This provides a valuable opportunity to express understanding, and to respond to the views of others in a supportive context.

Rainbow groups

A way of ensuring that children experience working alongside a range of others is to give each child in a group a number, or a colour. When the group has worked together, all the children of the same number or colour form new groups to compare what they have done.

Envoys

Often, in group work, the teacher is concerned that she/he will be under pressure from many different directions. Envoying helps children to find help and support without necessarily having recourse to the teacher. If a group needs to check something, or to obtain information, one of the group can be sent as an 'envoy' to the library, or book corner, or another group, and will then report back. Another use is to ask groups to send an envoy to a different group to explain what they have done, obtain responses and suggestions, and bring them back to the group.

Listening triads

This strategy encourages children, in groups of three, to take on the roles of talker, questioner or recorder. The talker explains or comments on an issue or activity. The questioner prompts and seeks clarification. The recorder makes notes, and at the end of the (brief) time, gives a report of the conversation. Next time the roles are changed.

Critical friends

A group member is responsible for observing the ways in which the group works together. Using a simple guide list (which children can devise), the observer watches and listens as the children work. This information is then discussed by the group. This helps children to develop their own evaluative strategies.

Cooperative forms of teaching quicken and deepen learning, and enhance a wide range of cognitive abilities. In particular:

- The model enhances certain higher cognitive abilities, in particular the capacity to form and reform concepts and transfer knowledge across domains.
- The model helps students develop the basic skills of memorisation. The capacity to memorise, hold and recall information is much enhanced.
- The model creates a cohesive context for learning that supports both able and less able students alike.
- The model encourages positive feelings among members, reduces loneliness and alienation, builds relationships and provides affirmative views of other people.

Effective group work involves an agreed set of ground rules that are based on self-respect for individuals and directed at creating efficient working patterns. These ground rules are negotiated as part of an introductory all-class session and refined by each group afterwards to suit their particular concerted needs. Framed as negatives or positives these 'commandments' should establish norms of civilised and democratic behaviour and if developed collaboratively will be accepted and followed more readily. The rules should be simple, reasonable and just. They include, for example:

- No one should interrupt another.
- No one should abuse another.
- No one should ignore another.
- Criticism must be justified and evidenced.
- Different opinions should be respected.
- Praise should be given.
- All members should offer help and share knowledge.

For cooperative methods of learning to be effective, they have to be planned, implemented and monitored very carefully. An ideological commitment to the idea is not enough and, indeed, can result in poorly-conceived group activities which may quickly deteriorated. While cooperative methods have an enormous potential for encouraging success in the classroom, this is unlikely to be the outcome unless they are introduced in a systematic and coordinated way. Facilitating effective small group learning means helping group members perceive the importance of working together and interacting in helpful ways. As seen in the following section, this can be accomplished by incorporating the five basic elements into all small group experiences (Johnson and Johnson 1993). Ultimately, these elements become tools for solving problems associated with group work.

Syntax of the Cooperative Group Work Teaching Model

There are a wide range of strategies that comprise the cooperative group work teaching model. They are all however underpinned by the following principles that comprise the syntax of this model of teaching (Johnson and Johnson 1993).

Positive interdependence – when all members of a group feel connected to each other in the accomplishment of a common goal. All individuals must succeed for the group to succeed.

Individual accountability – holding every member of the group responsible to demonstrate the accomplishment of the learning.

Face-to-face interaction – when group members are in close proximity to each other and enter into a dialogue with each other in ways that promote continued progress.

Social skills – human interaction skills that enable groups to function effectively (e.g. taking turns, encouraging, listening, giving help, clarifying, checking, understanding, probing). Such skills enhance communication, trust, leadership, decision-making, and conflict management.

Processing – when group members assess their collaborative efforts and target improvements.

Elaboration of the Cooperative Group Work Teaching Model

In this elaboration of the cooperative group work teaching model the 'Student Teams Achievement Divisions' (STAD) strategy is outlined (Slavin 1994). This involves four stages:

1. *Teacher instruction.* The teacher explains what students are going to learn in the lesson and why it is important. After reviewing prerequisite skills the teacher introduces the topic and aims to arouse interest with an intriguing demonstration or a real-life problem. In developing the topic

the teacher focuses on meaning and understanding and not just memorisation, and demonstrates the skills and the concepts, underpinning the verbal with the illustrative. Good practice at this stage includes:

- Frequently assessing student understanding through questions.
- Frequently explaining why answers are correct or not.
- Carefully moving from concept to concept.
- Maintaining pace by eliminating interruptions, reducing the number of questions and moving rapidly through material.

2. *Team study.* In teams, students work on the material presented in worksheet or fact-sheet form. Only two copies of the worksheet are provided per team, thus encouraging team-mates to work together. The teacher emphasises the cooperative nature of the activity. Teams must make sure that everyone knows enough to answer the test questions that will follow the activity. Worksheets and fact-sheets are for studying, not copying. Answers to questions should be rehearsed with team members and checked against any answers provided by the teacher. Questions should first be put to the team not the teacher. The rule is 'Ask Three Before Me'. During this stage the teacher circulates, prompting, encouraging, monitoring endeavour; sitting with teams, observing and listening to progress reports.

3. *Test.* In the third phase students are tested. The purpose of the test is to see what students have learnt individually and to calculate the extent performance has improved. Hence, collaboration is allowed. Students work on their own and in a new seating plan achieved by moving numbered students around the room – all number 1s remain, number 2s move round one group, etc.

    Team performance is measured according to improvement scores. In this scheme a baseline score is best established by the pre-test, post-test method. Students are tested before they have learnt something (at the beginning of the lesson) and then immediately after the learning sequence. This means each team member is competing not against another but against their own standard. In the STAD model the pre-test is usually delivered at the start of the lesson. In some subjects there may alternative ways of establishing a baseline score by which to measure improvement. In language and maths for instance, previous test scores or homework grades converted into numeric values might replace the pre-test concept.

4. *Team recognition.* Rates of improvement are converted into points on a sliding scale so that full marks gets 30 points. This method means that a negative score is never recorded and guarantees each member has the satisfaction of contributing something positive to the group. Team scores are calculated as an average, and rewards – merits or certificates – are awarded. In addition, the possibility of graduated success through premier status to super, to top status lures teams to greater and greater efforts.

Activity 4.1: Using Collaborative Teaching Techniques

Aim

- To examine alternative strategies for promoting student collaboration and cooperation.

Step 1

Within your department or subject area conduct an audit of existing practice of using cooperative activities across the department (see pro forma below). Afterwards, as a group discuss the implications of the findings.

Existing practice of using cooperative activities

Strategy	Often	Sometimes	Rarely
Dyads and Triads: Think–pair–share			
Twos to fours			
Brainstorming			
Snowballing			
Jigsawing			
Numbered heads			
Spontaneous group discussion			
Cooperative review			

Step 2

In pairs consider a recent lesson where cooperative group work was included. Estimate its success against the five principal criteria outlined below.

- **Positive interdependence:** the group depends on all its members to get its task done. All have a role to fulfil and a task to achieve.
- **Individual accountability:** all members have a responsibility to work for and with the group and have to account for what they do.
- **Face-to-face interaction:** students must discuss with others.
- **Social development:** students acquire the skills of listening, encouraging, explaining, organising.
- **Reflection:** students are encouraged to think about what they have done and understand the process of their learning.

In the light of your analysis, what changes could be made to the lesson to improve the cooperative activity?

Step 3

Consider where group work might be effectively implemented in your schemes of work. Identify a block of work that would benefit from the introduction of appropriate cooperative strategies.

CHAPTER 5

Inductive Teaching

Inductive teaching is a model of teaching that encourages students to build, test and to use categories. It nurtures logical thinking and allows students of all abilities to process information effectively.

Vignette

A Year 10 class is being introduced to different styles of portrait painting as part of their GCSE course. Initially the teacher gives each individual an A4 hand-out containing numbered photographs of different kinds of portraits. The portraits represent a range of styles and are from different centuries. For 5 minutes, the teacher gets the class to look at the photographs individually. The class is then divided into pairs and the teacher instructs each pair to categorise the portraits by grouping certain photographs together using the photograph numbers to group the categories. The pairs set about this task by placing the portraits into groups and giving each category a name. The teacher makes it clear that some portraits could be placed in several categories. She also reassures the students by telling them that any categories which can be named and justified are acceptable.

After 15 minutes or so, the teacher pauses this activity and asks several of the pairs to share their classification with the whole-class and their reasons for classifying the portraits in this way. The pairs offer a series of numbers that are written up by the teacher for the whole-class to view. While this is happening, other students look at their own classifications to ascertain whether they have reached similar conclusions or not. Having provided a set of numbers the other students are then asked by the teacher to guess the rationale behind the classification. One pair offers '17th century' as one category, while another offers 'cubism' as a category. Eventually the initiators of the classification are asked to tell the class why they grouped the data together and the teacher helps the whole-class look for links between the data chosen.

After several pairs have provided their categories and the class has worked out their reasons for grouping the data together, the teacher then hands each pair some additional photographs of portraits. The pairs are then asked to reconsider their categories with respect to the new data. The students are given time to allocate the new data within existing categories, or to recategorise the whole data set. Once they have completed this task the teacher once again asks selected pairs to share their classification and the labels they have given each category.

The teacher lists the different categories and asks the students to add any categories not represented by the list. The teacher then asks the students to choose one category and to paint a portrait in this style.

Description of the Inductive Teaching Model

The inductive teaching model is a powerful way of helping students to learn how to construct knowledge. The model focuses directly upon intellectual capability and is intended to assist students in the process of mastering large amounts of information. Within teaching there are numerous occasions when students are required to sort and classify data. However, in many cases the sorting process is viewed as an end in itself. Students are usually required to understand the 'one correct way of classifying'. Teachers know that there are many ways of classifying but often they choose just one for simplicity. The inductive method allows students to understand a variety of classifications in a structured way that includes a variety of teaching techniques within one method. Without opportunity for reclassification or hypothesising, learning potential is limited and the development of higher order thinking is restricted.

The inductive model of teaching consists of a number of discrete phases that cannot be rushed or omitted. Inductive inquiries are rarely brief because the very nature of the inquiry requires students to think deeply. The inductive model in synthesis is the collecting and sifting of information in order to construct categories, or labels. This process requires students to engage with the data and seek to produce categories in which to allocate the data. It requires them to generate hypotheses based upon this allocation and to test out these hypotheses by using them to guide subsequent work.

The flow of the inductive model involves:

- data collection/presentation.

Identifying and enumerating the data relevant to a topic or a problem.

- examining and enumerating data.

Grouping individual data or items into categories that have common attributes.

- classifying data and labelling.

Interpreting the data and developing labels for the categories. This also involves identifying and exploring critical relationships and making inferences, creating hypotheses and converting categories to skills.

The inductive teaching model follows a sequence of six phases. In the first phase students are presented with data sets and required to sort the data into categories. The data sets are derived from a subject area and are intended to facilitate learning about a particular topic or theme. The data sets can be assembled by the teacher in advance of the lesson or collected by the students with guidance from the teacher. If assembled by the teacher, the data sets will be prepared with certain concepts in mind. To engage students in this model, teachers need to begin by presenting data sets to them and in subsequent lessons encouraging students to create and generate their own data sets. It is important that students have experience of the inductive model in all its phases and have success in learning with this model before embarking upon more sophisticated and complicated data sets.

To be really effective, data classification needs to occur several times. The initial phase of the classification is particularly important because this is where new concepts are generated and applied. Following this initial phase, additional data or new information may be added that will require some reclassification or refinement of the categories. Adding new data means that concepts are challenged requiring students to think again about their initial classification. Through this iterative process students obtain control over the data and can understand related concepts more readily.

Inductive teaching increases students' ability to form concepts and to create linkages between different concepts. It also enables students to have a wider perspective on the topic in question and to think more broadly about the subject matter. Another, important aspect of the inductive model is the collective nature of the inquiry and the group responsibility to contribute to the compilation of categories. By allowing individuals to share their ideas with the whole-class, different perspectives on the same data and challenges to thinking are inevitable. There are many other advantages to the use of the model:

- it engages students in higher order thinking;
- it involves variety in that the stages are taught in different ways so it supports a variety of learning styles;
- once the data has been prepared, it can easily be kept from one year to another;
- once the data has been prepared, it is easy to share among members of staff and across different schools;
- providing teachers keep to the stages of the model, it provides a varied and stimulating way to learn.

Syntax of the Inductive Teaching Model

Phase One: Identify the domain

• Establish the focus and boundaries of the initial inquiry.
• Clarify the long-term objectives.

Phase Two: Collect, present and enumerate data

• Assemble and present the initial data set.
• Enumerate and label the items of data.

Phase Three: Examine data

• Thoroughly study the items in the data set and identify their attributes.

Phase Four: Form concepts by classifying

• Classify the items in the data set and share the results.
• Add data to the set.
• Reclassification occurs, possibly many times.

Phase Five: Generate and test hypotheses

• Examine the implications of differences between categories.
• Classify categories, as appropriate.
• Reclassify in two-way matrices, as well as by correlations, as appropriate.

Phase Six: Consolidate and transfer

• Search for additional items of data in resource material.
• Synthesize by writing about the domain, using the categories.
• Convert categories into skills.
• Test and consolidate skills through practice and application.

(*Source*: Joyce and Calhoun 1998)

Elaboration of the Inductive Teaching Model

A Year 10 class has been considering global population issues in their GCSE geography course. One of the major learning outcomes of this topic is generating the understanding that the population characteristics of any country are linked to other socio-economic factors. The use of a series of lessons using the inductive method allows students to appreciate this relationship in some depth. In the first lesson the teacher puts the class into groups of four. The students are told that they have to collect information about 16 countries from an atlas and record it using a set pro forma (see opposite).

Information about countries

1. Name of country	
2. Continent	
3. Population total in millions	
4. Population density per km²	
5. Birth rate per 1000	
6. Death rate per 1000	
7. Life expectancy	
8. Percentage of the population living in towns (urban)	
9. GNP per head in USA $	
10. Population per doctor	

During the lesson, all groups collect the data for specified countries using the pro forma and complete this by the end of the lesson. The second lesson involves the groups putting the countries into groups by using their own sets of criteria. The students are given a sheet (see sheet headed Global population) to record their categories. As the exercise progresses, it becomes apparent that certain strategies can be combined (e.g. death rate and GNP per head).

Global population

Your name: _____

Names of the other people in your group:

        _____

        _____

        _____

As you put the countries into groups, record your decisions on this sheet.

Countries in the group?	Main reason for putting the countries into this group?	What else do the countries have in common?

On each card the country is given a letter code, which is useful for sorting the data and discussing the categories that are established. Fifteen minutes before the end of the lesson, the teacher asks each group in turn to agree upon their 'best' category (i.e. one they are most pleased with or they think other groups will not be able to guess). The last ten minutes of the lesson involves each group giving their 'best' category to the teacher, who records it on the board. All the other groups have to suggest why these countries have been categorised in this way by the group. Following this discussion, the group is asked for their particular rationale for putting the data together. Towards the end of the lesson the teacher picks out some of the categories based on population criteria (not socio-economic indicators) which point towards three basic groupings:

- More Economically Developed Countries (MEDCs) – slow rate of population growth
- Less Economically Developed Countries (LEDCs) – fast rate of population growth
- Middle group – moderate rate of population growth.

These groupings provide the basis for the next lesson which covers the generation of hypotheses. Using the data on the cards, and the teacher's help in class discussion, the class comes up with examples of hypotheses which the teacher records on the board, e.g. using the pro forma overleaf and statements such as:

- Countries where the population is growing very fast are .... in the .... continent.
- Countries with a fast growing population tend to have/be .... (social and economic indicators are included here) because ....

Examples of countries where the population is growing fast:

These countries usually have: **Factors**	**Because**

These countries are called (*delete what does not apply*)
LEDCs   MEDCs   This stands for_____

The students are requested to do the same for MEDCs, with less directed help from the teacher.

Examples of countries where the population is growing slowly:	
These countries usually have: **Factors**	**Because**

These countries are called (*delete what does not apply*)
LEDCs   MEDCs   This stands for_____

As a class activity or a homework topic, students are asked to write a paragraph on:

- MEDCs
- LEDCs.

Aims

- To explore different ways in which data might be assembled for inductive teaching purposes.
- To consider the features of data sets and how they might be presented in different subject contexts.

Step 1

Data sets are essentially a collection of information that can be organised according to concepts defined by the particular subject, theme or topic. Within inductive teaching, the responsibility of the teacher is to present students with a data set that has some underlying conceptual framework. Students then have to take responsibility either individually, in pairs or in groups for creating categories and sorting the data accordingly.

Within subject areas divide into pairs and think of a topic, or a particular theme that could be readily converted into a data set. Consider the following questions:

1. Who would compile the data set? (It needs to be common to the whole class.)

2. How could it be made accessible to weak readers?

3. What prompts would you give students (if any) in order to sort the data?

4. What additional data might be offered to students?

5. What extension activities would you request of students?

Step 2

Consider the following data set. In groups of four, sort the data into categories through discussion and negotiation. Group the data using the numbers that appear on the card. For example, numbers 1, 5, 10, 15 are activities associated with student centered learning.

Interactive data set

A set of data is collected by the students, or presented to them. **1.**	The teacher presents the topic to be explored and sets the context. **2.**
Students develop a hypothesis. Predictions are made and tested with further data. **3.**	The teacher organises the students into roles and procedures, and explains goal of the exercise. **4.**
The teacher presents a problem situation. **5.**	The teacher conducts a debriefing session with the students. **6.**
The students discuss common attributes and sort the data into categories. **7.**	Labels are developed for the categories by identifying critical features. **8.**
Further data may be collected or given to test the categories. Data may be re-categorised. **9.**	The students participate in the game or simulation. The teacher acts as referee and coach **10.**
A problem is formulated and structured with teacher guidance. **11.**	Practice recalling the material until it is completely learned. **12.**

The students organise what needs to be done to study the problem. **13.**	Develop mental images through ridiculous associations, exaggerations. **14.**
Information to be learned is discussed and manipulated through lists, underlining, etc. **15.**	After the discussion of progress, further investigations may be carried out, perhaps in different student groups. **16.**
Students and teacher discuss progress. The teacher develops their skills of cooperative investigation. **17.**	Material is then made familiar through making connections with key-words, link-words. **18.**
Independent and group study tasks are carried out. **19.**	

| Step 3 | Once all groups have completed the task then each group shares one category without explanation. Other groups compare their list of numbers and selected categories and try to guess why the data was categorised together. |

| Step 4 | The groups are then asked to reconsider their categories, with the addition of extra data. Groups are also asked to draw some conclusions from the data set and to reflect upon the process of learning inductively by considering: |

- How they approached the task.
- How they sorted the data.
- How they constructed the categories.
- Whether they changed any categories.
- What they learned and how they learned.
- What they can hypothesise about teaching inductively.

| Step 5 | The groups consider how different subject areas could use inductive teaching and what types of data sets would be most appropriate. This is shared at a plenary session. |

CHAPTER 6

Synectics

Synectics is a model of teaching that encourages students to make connections between concepts and to produce new ways of thinking about a topic or idea.

Vignette

A Year 11 GCSE English class are studying Arthur Miller's play *A View from the Bridge,* and are asked to think about the character and personality of Beatrice Carbone.

The teacher asks the class to describe Beatrice and her personality by listing key ideas and adjectives, e.g. mother, wife, understanding, confused, angry, etc. Then students are asked to use direct analogy to think creatively about the situation or topic. Students are asked to select a machine that has Beatrice's qualities, as they have identified them (e.g. a washing machine, a vacuum cleaner, a dishwasher, an electric cooker).

The teacher then asks the students for the machine that would make the strangest comparison between it and Beatrice? The students share their ideas and the class vote on the best analogy. The students then describe how this machine works by listing its functions and characteristics (e.g. electric cooker).

Students are asked to imagine they are the machine (e.g. electric cooker); and to write about how it feels to be that machine. For example:

'I don't have any control over my life. I have to wait until she switches me on. I get frustrated!'
'One minute I'm cold, the next I'm too hot. I'm unpredictable.'
'I'm lonely, as I never see another cooker.'

Students are asked to select two words that conflict with each other from the earlier exploration of being a machine; for example:

'frustrated love'
'hungry greed'
'proud loner'.

Having generated a list of these words, they are asked to select the best (e.g. 'frustrated love').

Students are asked to use this phrase (i.e. 'frustrated love') and apply it to the animal world; for example:

'A bird in a cage looking out at wild birds singing.'
'A horse in a horsebox being driven away from a wild horse running free in a field.'

The teacher then returns the class to the original problem and draws upon the creativity generated in the lesson. Students are asked to write about Beatrice's personality, using the various analogies they have generated; for example:

'Beatrice is trapped in an infinite spiral of helplessness.'
'She has a feeling of suppressed rage.'
'She is a bird in a cage who is scared by the truth.'
'She is trapped inside a world she does not want to be in ... she has frustrated love.'

Description of the Synectics Teaching Model

Synectics as a model of teaching aims to increase the creativity of both individuals and groups. The model is premised upon using creative thought to generate new and different ways of thinking about an issue or a problem. A main strategy within this model is the use of analogies to increase students' creative expression, empathy and insight. The model stresses the relationship between creative activity and a deeper understanding of ideas. It emphasises the use of metaphoric associations to create new perspectives on a topic or issue. However, the model is not confined to only those subjects that most readily encompass the use of metaphoric thinking such as English or drama but can be used within all subject areas to promote higher order thinking. Within all fields (i.e. the arts, the sciences, engineering) creative processes are used to foster the same intellectual processes, although in science this may be called 'innovation' and in engineering it may be termed 'invention'.

Synectics offers a different way of problem-solving that is the antithesis of logical thought. The model requires students to think in a variety of ways that may be considered illogical or ridiculous. In order to move students away from learned solutions and the usual ways of thinking about a problem, synectics uses three types of analogy to encourage creative thought. For further information see Joyce and Weil (1996) and Joyce *et al.* (1997).

Direct analogy requires a simple comparison of two objects or concepts. For example, students may be asked in a biology lesson 'how is blood like a waterfall?' or 'why is skin like glass?' The main purpose of this comparison is to elicit features that present both concepts in an extended and new way. By thinking about the way in which the two elements or ideas are similar and different, allows students to be creative and imaginative. It also allows new connections to be made between quite different concepts.

Personal analogy requires students to empathise with the ideas or problems to be compared. Students are encouraged to express how they feel as if they were immersed in the problem. The purpose of personal analogy is to encourage empathy and involvement. It requires students to imagine the situation or problem from a perspective other than their own.

Compressed conflict requires students to provide a two-word description of an object, person or situation. The words selected have to be opposites, or seem to contradict each other. The aim of the two-word description is to compress meaning by using only two frames of reference with respect to a single concept. This task requires creative thinking and is another way of helping students to make new connections between ideas and to engage in higher order thinking.

The synectic model of teaching has six discrete phases, although certain components such as personal analogy may be used in isolation within a lesson to generate creative thinking.

In the initial phase of the model students are asked to write a paragraph about a particular topic, e.g. the life cycle of a fish. On completion of this task they are then asked to create some *direct analogies,* e.g. How is water like a feather? How is a fish like a bullet? How are dead leaves like scales on a fish? The purpose of this phase is to generate some creative ideas about the topic.

The third phase requires students to engage in a *personal analogy,* e.g. imagine you are a fish swimming away from a predator – how do you feel? In this phase students generate responses, e.g. scared, desperate, threatened. They are then asked to use these responses to generate some *compressed conflicts* that have an implicit tension or incongruity, e.g. 'scared bravery', 'desperate confidence', 'threatened security'. In Phase Five of the model they are asked to chose two of the word pairs and to engage in a direct analogy, e.g. What would it be like to be 'desperately confident'? What would 'scared bravery' feel like?

In the last phase of the model the students are asked to write another paragraph about the life cycle of the fish and to incorporate, where possible, the ideas they have generated from the different types of metaphorical thought. Through encouraging students to capture some of their creative writing in the rewriting of the paragraph, ideas are extended and a deeper understanding of the topic is achieved.

The most effective use of synectics develops over time. In the short term it can extend students' thinking about different concepts and problems, but used repeatedly it will engender creative thinking skills that will improve students' learning generally. Synectics helps students to develop their creative capacity and to refine their creative thinking skills for use in all subject areas. It helps students stretch their ideas and to reformulate them in ways that contribute to creative thinking and higher order thinking skill development.

An effective synectics lesson involves careful classroom management. The following are important requirements for an effective synectics lesson:

- students must be able to see the board easily – this is more important than sitting behind a desk;
- it is easier if students have no equipment on their desks;
- students do not need to be told what they are doing (the processes seem very complex) but they do need to know *why* they are doing it;
- the teacher needs to explain that the process will seem odd but encourage them not to question it; the extreme ideas are often the most useful;
- students need to understand that thinking is working even though they will not be doing any writing – worth reinforcing in depth even if the teacher thinks this has been covered before;
- the teacher will need to emphasise that everyone in the class will be expected to contribute, and to listen to each other.

Syntax of the Synectic Teaching Model

Phase One: Description of the present condition

Phase Two: Direct analogy

Phase Three: Personal analogy

Phase Four: Compressed conflict

Phase Five: Direct analogy

Phase Six: Re-examination of the original task

(*Source*: Joyce *et al.* 1997)

Elaboration of the Synectic Teaching Model

Within a social studies lesson Year 10 students are placed into groups of five. They asked to write a paragraph about career women in India. They do this individually and then share their paragraphs with other members of their group (Phase One). The students are then asked to respond to some direct analogies written on the board by the teacher (Phase Two); for example:

'How is a feather like a butterfly?' (attractive, soft, flight, pursued)
'How are scissors like a cactus?' (sharp, sting)
'How is a snake like a pillow?' (slippery, gives you nightmares)

The students are then asked to make personal analogies with prompts from the teacher (Phase Three); for example:

'Be a tiger. Good morning tigers how do you feel?' (grand, kingly, hungry, untrustworthy)
'Be a feather. Tell me about yourself?' (no worries, fragile, flighty)

Using the words they have generated, students are then asked to construct work pairs that seem to fight each other (Phase Four); for example:

'majestically greedy'
'carefully threatened'
'fragile independent.'

They are then required to make direct analogies between these words (Phase Five); for example:

'What is an example of fragile independence?'
'How might you be majestically greedy?'

Having written about these direct analogies and discussed them with others in their group, the students are then requested to write another paragraph on 'career women' using the point of view of one the direct analogies (Phase Six); for example:

'A career woman can be majestically greedy if she wants to succeed in business. She has to be powerful but fragile in order to gain respect.'

Participation in synectics invariably creates a unique shared experience that fosters interpersonal understanding and a sense of community. Members learn about one another as each person reacts to a common event or experience. Each thought or idea, no matter how prosaic, is valued for its potential contribution to creative thought. Everyone's ideas are valued and there is a sense of 'playfulness' within synectic activity that encourages participation from even the most timid students in the class.

Aims

- To consider strategies based on synectic procedures.
- To consider the way in which synectics could be applied in different subject areas.

Step 1   Within synectics the strategy of creating something new is important as it helps students to see things in unfamiliar ways. To practise this strategy teachers are placed into groups of four or five and asked to consider the syntax of the model.

Syntax of the Model

Phase One: Description of the present condition

Phase Two: Direct analogy

Phase Three: Personal analogy

Phase Four: Compressed conflict

Phase Five: Direct analogy

Phase Six: Re-examination of the original task

Teachers are then each asked to write a paragraph about 'being a teacher' and to share this paragraph with the group. Following this phase they will be required to suggest some direct analogies that other groups could use, e.g. a gardener, a guide, a mentor. These are recorded and handed to the nearest group on completion of the task. Each group then considers the analogies they are given and use them to make comparisons. These comparisons are written down and handed back to the group that provided the direct analogies. Within the groups, one or two analogies are used in a personal sense, i.e. the group members become the analogy. Using these descriptions, the group then suggest several compressed conflicts. The group decide upon the best example and use this to form another direct analogy. Finally, the group rewrite their paragraphs and compare them with the initial writing undertaken at the start of the session.

Step 2   All groups judge the qualities of the final paragraphs written and generate a list of 'quality features' about teaching arising from each. These are shared in a plenary feedback session. The groups discuss ways in which synectics has advanced their thinking.

Step 3

Once all groups have completed the task each group considers the following questions and records its responses for subsequent sharing with other groups.

Could synectics be used in my subject area?
What topics could be enhanced by using this approach?
What barriers might there be?
How might these be overcome?
Are there opportunities for some subjects to use this model more than others? If so why?

Creating the Conditions for Teaching and Learning – © IQEA

Step 4   In subject areas, teachers plan one synectics lesson each and agree how they will build it into their teaching across the subject area. They complete the following grid which is then photocopied and shared with all subject areas:

Subject area plan for using synectics

Year group	Teacher	Topic	When/Which class?	Intended learning outcomes	Extension activities

CHAPTER 7

Concept Attainment

Concept attainment is a model of teaching that expands students' ability to acquire, control and remember information.

Vignette

In a Year 8 English lesson students are given 20 sentences to compare. Each sentence is labelled either A or B. Examples of these sentences are as follows:

A. The sun was an *orb of light.*   B. The sun shone brightly.

A. The moon was a *diamond of the night.*   B. The moon looked like a diamond.

A. *Ice-cool pain stabbed* at his heart.   B. It was a pain like frozen ice.

The students are told to individually scrutinise the sentences and to pay particular attention to the words in italics. They are also told that the 'A' sentences are positive exemplars and that the 'B' sentences are negative exemplars. They are also told that the positive exemplars have something in common in the work they do in the sentence.

The negative examples do not have these features. Students are asked to make notes about what they believe the exemplars have in common. Again, this is undertaken individually. The teacher then presents more sets of examples and asks students whether they still have the same idea. Examples continue to be presented until most of the students have an idea that they think will withstand questioning. Students are asked to raise their hands if they are sure they know what the sentences have in common. At this point, the teacher asks individual students to provide their explanation. One student might say 'The B sentences are all very descriptive', another suggests that the sentences 'describe things as if

---

they were other things'. Another student suggests that the A sentences 'are more accurate descriptions as they say what the things are like'.

As other students offer their ideas, it gradually becomes clear that the A sentences are metaphors. The teacher uses the ideas offered by the students to illuminate what a metaphor is and how it is used. The teacher then provides the name of the concept (metaphor) and asks the students to agree on a definition. The teacher concludes the lesson by asking the students to share their thinking on how they arrived at the concept and to describe how they used the information given to arrive at a conclusion.

Description of the Concept Attainment Model of Teaching

Concept attainment has been defined as the search for and listing of attributes that can be used to distinguish exemplars from non-exemplars of various categories. In the inductive model of teaching the emphasis is on building and forming concepts. Consequently, students decide the categories on which to construct the concepts that they subsequently use. In contrast, concept attainment requires students to ascertain concepts that are already formed and defined. This is achieved by asking students to compare and contrast examples (called exemplars) that contain the characteristics (called attributes) of the concept with examples that do not contain those attributes.

Concept attainment provides an opportunity for both students and teachers to reflect upon and analyse thought processes and to evaluate how thinking can be improved. This model of teaching provides practice for students in reasoning and logical thought processes. Research has shown that students learn how to attain concepts through practice, and concept attainment is an important means of providing such practice. The more students practise manipulating and pre-empting concepts, the more effectively they attain and can apply conceptual knowledge. It has been shown that concept attainment is a far more effective way of teaching concepts as students engage with the ideas much more deeply. In addition, concept attainment allows students to play with ideas and to recognise the possibility of alternative and opposing perspectives. This reinforces the importance of tolerance of ambiguity and the possibility of competing explanations.

The concept attainment model of teaching has three discrete phases:

• The first phase involves presenting data to students in the form of 'example' and 'non-example'.

This data is presented to students in pairs. At first only a few examples are given to the students to enable them to focus upon the differences and similarities. This information may be in the form of events, people, descriptions or illustrations. The subject area and the concepts that teachers wish to elicit from the students will largely dictate the form of the data. On receipt of this data the students are told that there is one common idea that all the positive examples contain and that this idea is not present in the negative examples. The students are then set the task of developing a hypothesis about the nature of this idea and to ascertain this from a comparison of the positive and negative examples. The students are asked to name their idea and to define its essential attributes. This phase is undertaken individually.

- In the second phase the students test out their understanding (attainment) of the idea (concept).

This is achieved firstly by providing additional examples and allowing students to re-examine their idea. This is further tested by students identifying additional unlabelled examples of the concept and finally by generating their own examples. At this point the teacher asks the students to share their hypotheses and confirms the correct concept along with its key attributes.

- In the third phase of the concept attainment model, students are asked to consider how they arrived at their conclusion and to revisit their thinking processes when they analysed the data.

In reflecting upon their process of thought with others in the classroom students are more able to evaluate their ability to reason and to think logically. With the teacher's assistance students are encouraged to consider the effectiveness of their own thinking strategies.

Syntax of the Concept Attainment Model of Learning and Teaching

Phase 1: Presentation of data and identification of the concept

- The teacher presents labelled examples.
- Students compare attributes in positive and negative examples.
- Students generate and test hypotheses.
- Students state a definition according to the essential attributes.

Phase 2: Testing attainment of the concept

- Students identify additional unlabelled examples as *yes* or *no*.
- The teacher confirms hypotheses, names concept and restates definitions according to essential attributes.
- Students generate examples.

Phase 3: Analysis of thinking strategies

- Students describe thoughts.
- Students discuss role of hypotheses and attributes.
- Students discuss type and number of hypotheses.

(*Source*: Joyce *et al.* 1997)

Elaboration   Within an economics lesson the concepts of demand and supply are being taught to Year 9 students. Twenty sets of data are used to illustrate the concepts.

The teacher presents pairs of attributes – some illustrate positive exemplars and some negative ones. After two or three pairs the teacher asks each student individually to write down why those which are positive exemplars have been put together (that is, what these attributes have in common).

The teacher presents a few more pairs and asks students if these fit their concept. If they do not, can they rewrite their concept? The teacher then presents some attributes individually and asks students to place them in the positive or negative column. She/he does this by asking the whole class to vote on 'How many of you would put this in the positive column?' 'How many in the negative?' The teacher goes through several attributes at this stage. Once the class gets to the point where all (or virtually all) are agreeing, she/he asks the students to discuss in pairs what they think the teacher 'has in mind'.

The teacher asks students about their ideas on the nature of the concept and confirms their views by restating the definition using the first few examples in the positive column. Following this the teacher could give students an attribute in the negative column and ask them to rewrite it so that it can be put in the positive column, or the teacher could ask the students to generate other positive attributes for the concept.

Activity 7.1: Concept Attainment

Aims

- To consider how exemplars and non-exemplars are devised and used within the classroom context.
- To consider the way in which concept attainment could be applied in different subject areas.

Step 1

In their subject areas teachers consider the types of topics that could be taught using concept attainment. The following list is provided as the basis for discussion and teachers in each subject area are asked to add further examples. This information is then shared in a feedback session.

English	Metaphoric writing Prejudice Alliteration
Science	Pure compounds Genetic variation Continuous variation Excretory products Parts of the body
History	Propaganda based on visual sources Primary and secondary sources Bias based on written statements
Geography	Population data associated with more and less economically developed countries Hydrography shapes – factors which result in flooding and those which do not Weathering/erosion Coastal/river flooding Arable/pastoral farming

Step 2

Within subject area groupings teachers are asked to:

• Select a concept.

• Devise some positive and negative exemplars for the concept.

• Put them in priority order. The clearest ones should come first. Leave some for the students to place in the positive or negative column.

After completing this task teachers are asked to identify (a) any problems or barriers that they encountered during the task and (b) suggest ways in which the process of formulating exemplars and non-exemplars might be simplified (see pro forma).

Problems and how to overcome them

Problems/barriers	How to overcome them

Step 3   In mixed groups the teachers try out their exemplars using other members of the group as respondents.

Step 4   The group evaluate the effectiveness of different sets of exemplars.

CHAPTER 8

Assessment as a Tool for Learning

Introduction

The part assessment plays in how students learn, and learn to improve, depends on the way a school and its teachers regard learning. Researchers have identified two kinds of learning – *superficial* and *deep*. Rote-learning, for instance, is frequently cited as an example of superficial learning because it involves the passive reception of ideas, the disregard of the underlying ways knowledge is organised and a focus on the uncritical replication of data on demand. Deep-learning, on the other hand, develops the higher cognitive skills of understanding and conceptual expression, is actively engaged with content and enquiry, links evidence to conclusions and integrates new ideas with previous knowledge. In other words it makes students think for themselves. It makes learning *meaningful*, both in the sense of it being about understanding and meaning and in the sense that it is an important, valued (meaningful) activity for the student.

How students learn and how effectively they learn depends greatly on how they are assessed. There are four major ways in which assessment can help students improve their learning:

- Assessment can motivate students to learn by emphasising the achievable and developing self-confidence.

- Assessment helps students to know what to learn by providing feedback.

- Assessment helps students to learn how to learn by encouraging active (deep) learning, by guided use of learning strategies, by developing skills of self-appraisal, by developing the ability to apply knowledge in diverse contexts.

- Assessment helps students judge the effectiveness of their learning by developing review skills, by consolidating and transforming existing learning.

Such forms of assessment are referred to as *formative* and are concerned with meaningful or purposeful learning.

Though there are many forms of assessment not all are formative. It is only when evidence from assessment contributes to the learning process that it begins to influence learners' behaviour and attitudes. This is demonstrated in the example below.

Elaboration –
Electrochemistry

As part of a Scheme of Work for Science Key Stage 4 a class has been introduced to some of the basic aspects of matter in preparation for exploring the concepts of elements, compounds and mixtures and the nature of atomic structure. In the first session the concept of a *pure* substance is being discussed.

The teacher tells the class that they will have certain targets to attain after the lesson and that to do this successfully they must listen carefully, help each other and follow worksheet instructions.

The teacher then introduces the double lesson by reminding students of the concept of *substance*, that all matter is made up of particles and that substances fall into three categories – solids, liquids and gases. The aim of the lesson is to introduce the concepts of *pure* and *mixed* substances.

An OHP display shows four possible definitions of pure. It states:
A pure substance:

1. has nothing added.
2. is natural.
3. contains only one substance.
4. is the same throughout.

Each student has this list duplicated on the worksheet and with a partner is asked to add to these possible definitions if they can and then decide which definition meets the scientific notion of pure. Each pair is then asked to join with another to form teams of four and pool ideas. After five minutes discussion the teacher asks for contributions. The class decides the right answer.

The teacher then asks the class to look at the second section of the worksheet where a number of substances are listed. Pairs have to decide which are pure and which mixtures, and to describe in the case of mixtures what the other substances are. They then add three more substances of their own and decide on their category.

In the second half of the lesson students move on to the third section of the worksheet. They are told to read a relevant textbook section on the subject of mixtures and pure substances. The reading recaps on what the lesson has covered so far and takes students into new areas of knowledge and understanding. The worksheet itemises exactly what the student has to learn from the reading by dividing content into three categories – what 'must' be learnt, what 'should' be learnt and what 'could' be learnt.

Finally, the fourth part of the worksheet requires all students to answer a number of questions corresponding to the 'must', 'should' and 'could' categories of learning already outlined.

In their workbook students record these targets and complete their responses in classwork/homework. When the teacher marks the results she/he gauges achievement against the targets and recommends action accordingly. Thus, if a student capable of achieving all three targets only manages 'must' or misunderstands the basic concepts then remedial action is called for. For example, students might be asked to revise uncertain areas by using an interactive CD-ROM on *Elements, Compound and Mixtures* and completing the Revision Challenge at the end. Only when the student has achieved a target total of 200 points in this Revision round will the teacher be satisfied that concepts have been understood and merits deserved.

Additionally, the teacher's comments on this work might list other areas for improvement. These are presented as targets for the following piece of classwork or homework and must be copied down by the student as a reminder when starting the next assignment.

Principles and implementation of assessment

There are a number of principles that underlie any successful system of managing, developing and improving student learning through the use of formative assessment.

- *Diagnosis*. Before learning can be effectively managed, schools and teachers must have some basic and reliable evidence about their students' progress to date and levels of attainment. Assessment, both formal and informal, contributes to this first diagnostic phase of planned learning. Only when data from a variety of sources – test scores, reports, interviews, observation – has been collected and collated into a student 'profile' can a teaching team begin to adjust their teaching to student achievement and relate it to departmental or school goals. Thus, where initial investigations reveal students with deficiencies in communication skills, especially in writing, then a Science department might develop a variety of alternative ways of presenting and recording findings such as pro forma experiment reports or graphical modes or oral presentations that allow students to practise the skills of observation without feeling inept and losing self-confidence.

- *Goals*. Just as teachers need to know the student-learner, so they need to have a clear idea about learning objectives and how subject aims fit in with the school's overall policy on learning. Research on the effectiveness of formative assessment as a tool for improvement has noted that success comes when such assessment is integrated into a whole-school strategy on teaching and learning.

- *Diversity of method*. Formative assessment focuses on a range of learning skills, from the acquisition of basic number skills to the higher cognitive functions of conceptual understanding, analysis, knowledge transfer and application. Hence, a diverse range of assessment methods are needed. Whatever range of assessment methods is selected teachers will not only need to relate it to overall school directives but they must also relate it to the demands of the subject.

- *Shared criteria*. Identifying what a school wants students to achieve is a precondition for successful learning. To be effective, formative assessment must be criteria-referenced because such assessment tells students what they *can* do rather than where they are *in relation to the performance of others*. If part of the learning process is for students to take more and more responsibility for their own development then educating them in how asessment occurs is important. Any assessment practice must be based on the principle that the greater the degree of student participation the greater the potential improvement in learning.

- *Feedback*. Research on teaching and assessment highlights the importance of feedback in the learning process. Without it students do not know how well they are doing and do not know what to do to improve and close the gap between current attainment and desired attainment. Feedback is related to learner confidence and should, in a system of both formal and informal reward and approval, increase motivation and self-esteem. This kind of feedback has been termed *evaluative*.

- *Self-reflection*. Not only does formative assessment draw students into managing their own learning but it also helps develop meta-cognition, the capacity to be aware of one's own learning, to be objective and stand back and evaluate it. Any system of assessment should therefore build in periodic points where students are asked to reflect on their own performance and the ways in which they have learned and achieved.

The implementation of a formative assessment process in a school tends to go through the following phases:

- collection of data and analysis of the existing learning context within a subject or at a Key Stage;
- profile of students;
- produce learner profiles;
- establishing school-wide goals and integration with department/subject goals;
- introduction of diverse teaching methods;
- creation of a collaborative culture that favours effective formative modes of assessment;
- sharing of criteria;
- development of marking policies;
- feedback and targeting linked to achievement and progress;
- monitoring standards by focusing on selected areas.

Aim

- To explore the relationship between current assessment practice and learning, and identify possible areas for further development.

Step 1 As a department, conduct an assessment audit. Complete the following form, listing as many examples as you can under each heading.

Assessment evidence			
Consider the types of evidence that students might generate in the course of a unit of work			
Oral evidence	**Written evidence**	**Graphical evidence**	**Products**

- Which are most frequently produced in your lessons and why?
- Are they under-used in your lessons?
- Which are the most useful for assessment purposes?
- Are any more suited to some attainment targets than others; if so, why?

Creating the Conditions for Teaching and Learning – © IQEA

Step 2   To further review existing departmental practice concerning assessment
          practices complete the following questionnaire individually.

Assessment evidence

- Is marking thorough and rigorous enough?
  Response:

- Does marking routinely point out how students can improve their work?
  Response:

- How is under-achievement recognised?
  Response:

- Is target-setting a standard feature of departmental assessment routines?
  Response:

- Is self-assessment a feature of departmental practice?
  Response:

Step 3	Now share your individual response with another member of your department.

Step 4	As a department consider how far your assessment practice covers the areas outlined below.

Extent of assessment practice

Purpose	**Who**
Motivation	Teacher
Diagnosis	Student
Judgement	Other students
Discussion	
Targets	
Information	

What	**Evidence**
Skills	Observation
Knowledge	Written work
Understanding	Practical work
Attitudes	Oral/aural
Personal qualities	Graphical
	Product
	Test

Creating the Conditions for Teaching and Learning – © IQEA

Step 5

Actions to be taken

As a department what action do you propose to take as a result of the review?

CHAPTER 9

The Staff Development Imperative

A systematic and integrated approach to staff development, that focuses on the professional learning of teachers and establishes the classroom as an important centre for teacher development, is central to successful school improvement. Our experience suggests that staff development is the central strategy for supporting teachers as they engage in improvement activities. Attention to teacher learning has direct spin-offs in terms of student learning.

The research evidence that is available on the effectiveness of staff development initiatives is however far from encouraging. Despite all the effort and resources that have been utilised, the impact of such programmes in terms of improvements in teaching and better learning outcomes for students is rather disappointing (Joyce and Showers 1995). Fullan (1991) for example, provides a bleak picture of in-service initiatives that are poorly conceptualised, insensitive to the concerns of individual participants and, perhaps crucially, make little effort to help participants relate their learning experiences to their usual workplace conditions.

In stark contrast to this gloomy analysis the research evidence from successful schools demonstrates how they build infrastructures for staff development within their day-to-day arrangements (see for example, Joyce *et al.* 1999). In these schools portions of the week are devoted to discussion of teaching approaches, regular observation sessions, and on-site coaching. This is the case in the IQEA school improvement programme where staff development is directed specifically at assisting teachers expand their range of teaching repertoires.

These approaches to school-based staff development are based on the research of Joyce and Showers (1995) who identify a number of key training components which have much greater power when used in combination than when used alone. The major components of training are:

- presentation of theory or description of skill or strategy;
- modelling or demonstration of skills or models of teaching;

- practise in simulated settings;
- structured and open-ended feedback;
- coaching for application.

Joyce (1992) has also distinguished the best location of these various forms of staff development – either in the 'workshop' or the 'workplace'. The *workshop*, which is equivalent to the best practice on the traditional INSET course, is where we gain *understanding*, see *demonstrations* of the teaching strategy we may wish to acquire, and have the opportunity to *practise* them in a non-threatening environment. If however we wish to transfer those skills that the workshop has introduced us to back into the *workplace* – the classroom and school – then merely attending the workshop is insufficient. The research evidence is very clear that skill acquisition and the ability to transfer vertically to a range of situations requires 'on-the-job-support' (Joyce and Showers 1995). This implies changes to the workplace and the way in which we organise staff development in our schools. In particular this means the opportunity for *immediate and sustained practice, collaboration and peer coaching*, and *studying development and implementation*.

The paradox is that changes to the workplace cannot be achieved without, in most cases, drastic alterations in the ways in which schools are organised. Yet the transfer of teaching skills from INSET sessions to classroom settings will not occur without them. Successful schools pay careful attention to their workplace conditions. Consequently staff development is perhaps the most crucial of the enabling conditions for school improvement. Before discussing how schools organise themselves around supporting teaching and learning in the IQEA project, it may be helpful to look in more detail at the principles underlying the design of staff development.

The most effective design for staff development is based on an evolutionary model of teacher learning founded on the ideas of Joyce and Showers (1980a, 1995). The writers maintain that whether we teach ourselves or whether we learn from a training agent, the outcomes of training can be classified into the following levels of impact:

- *Awareness*. At the awareness level we realise the importance of an area and begin to focus on it. With inductive teaching for example, the road to competence begins with awareness of the nature of inductive teaching, its probable uses and how it fits into the curriculum.
- *Concepts and organised knowledge*. Concepts provide intellectual control over relevant content. Essential to inductive teaching is knowledge of inductive processes, of how learners at various levels of cognitive development respond to inductive teaching, and knowledge of concept formation.
- *Principles and skills*. Principles and skills are tools for action. At this level we learn the skills of inductive teaching: how to help students collect data, organise it, and build concepts and test them. We also acquire the skills for adapting to students who display varying levels of

ability to think inductively and for teaching them the skills they lack. At this level there is potential for action – we are aware of the area, can think effectively about it, and possess the skills to act.

- *Application and problem-solving.* Finally, we transfer the concepts, principles, and skills of inductive learning to the classroom. We begin to use the teaching strategy we have learned, integrate it into our style, and combine the strategy with others in our repertoire. Only after this fourth level has been reached can we expect to impact on the learning of students.

When these phases are related to Joyce and Showers' approach to training a training matrix is produced as seen in Figure 9.1.

Level of impact / Training method/ Component	A. General awareness of new skills	B. Organised knowledge of underlying concepts and theory	C. Learning of new skills	D. Application on the job
1. Presentation/ Description (e.g. lecture) of new skills	●			
2. Modelling the new skills (e.g. live or video demonstrations)	●	●		
3. Practise in simulated settings	●	●	●	
4. Feedback on performance in simulated or real settings	●	●	●	●
5. Coaching/ Assistance on the job	●	●	●	●

Figure 9.1 A training matrix based on the work of Joyce and Showers (1980a, 1995)
(● denotes evidence)

A key element in achieving such effects is the provision of in-classroom support, or in Joyce and Showers' term, 'peer coaching'. We have found in our own school improvement work that it is the facilitation of peer coaching that enables teachers to extend their repertoire of teaching skills and to transfer them from different classroom settings to others. In particular, we have found that peer coaching is helpful when:

• curriculum and teaching provide the content of staff development;
• the focus of the staff development represents a new practice for the teacher;
• workshops are designed to develop understanding and skill;
• school-based groups support each other to attain 'transfer of training'.

(Joyce *et al.* 1999)

From our experience, coaching contributes to transfer of training in five ways (Joyce *et al.* 1999). In particular teachers who are coached:

• generally practise new strategies more frequently and develop greater skill;
• use their newly learned strategies more appropriately than 'uncoached' teachers;
• exhibit greater long-term knowledge retention and skill regarding those strategies in which they have been coached;
• are much more likely than 'uncoached' teachers to teach new models of learning to their students;
• exhibit clearer understandings with regarding the purposes and uses of the new strategies.

During the implementation of this approach during our IQEA school improvement projects we have made refinements in the use of peer coaching to support student learning. We have found that when the refinements noted below are incorporated into a school improvement design, peer coaching can virtually assure 'transfer of training' for everyone. In particular:

• peer coaching teams of two or three are much more effective than larger groups;
• these groups are more effective when the entire staff is engaged in school improvement;
• peer coaching works better when the senior management team participate in training and practice;
• the effects are greater when formative study of student learning is embedded in the process.

Although peer coaching is an essential component of staff development, it also needs to be connected to other elements in order to form an effective school improvement strategy. As we shall see in the next chapter, the school improvement group is one way of facilitating this. The school improvement group represents the range of attitudes and experience of the staff, it is hierachical and normally consists of four to six members. It is this 'cadre' group that facilitates improvement activities within the school.

The main phases of activity that are facilitated by the cadre group are as follows:

Phase 1

- Consultation on IQEA.
- Teaching and learning becomes focus of development plan.
- Staff development is incorporated on the timetable.

Phase 2

- Whole-staff INSET on teaching strategies.
- Departmental groups collaborate on integrating teaching strategy into Schemes of Work.
- Cadre group support departmental groups on their teaching strategies.
- Departmental groups collaborate on integrating strategy into Schemes of Work.
- Partnership teaching/coaching.

Phase 3

- Curriculum tour – whole-staff INSET day.

Phase 4 and subsequently

- Departmental groups adopt a new range of teaching models and integrate them into their Schemes of Work.

During these phases the whole staff of the school are engaged on a range of staff development activities:

- Whole-staff INSET days on teaching and learning and school improvement planning, as well as curriculum tours to share the work done in departments or working groups.
- Inter-departmental meetings to discuss teaching strategies.
- Workshops run inside the school on teaching strategies by cadre group members and external support.
- Partnership teaching and peer coaching.

In addition cadre group members are involved in:

- Out of school training sessions on capacity building and teaching and learning.
- Planning meetings in school.
- Consultancy to school working groups.
- Observation and in-classroom support.

Our experience of working with school improvement groups suggests that simply belonging to the group is seen as a major staff development opportunity. This is because the cadre group's work quickly becomes a significant part of the school's improvement agenda.

Consequently, most cadre group members are busier and spend more time at school than they did. The motivation for the increase in commitment seems to spring from two sources. On the one hand, there is often a very real sense of 'making an impact' – actually influencing the quality of learning opportunities in the school, seeing changes, feeling that the school is meeting the learning needs of its students better. On the other, there is a heightened sense of professionalism. Different kinds of dialogue and discussion take place, more emphasis is placed on pedagogy, more sharing of practice develops, and a clearer sense of the professional challenges and achievements that teachers address daily develops.

As we see in the case studies in Chapter 10, those schools that have built an effective infrastructure for school improvement have found ways of linking the work of the school improvement group to the wider school community. For in the same way that the school improvement group is mutually supportive of one another, the school community makes a number of tacit commitments, too:

- To support each partnership in whatever way possible – time, resources, visits to centres of good practice, the adoption of recommendations, etc.

- To agree to remain informed about the progress of each area of enquiry in order to maintain collective ownership of the directions being travelled.

- To support the implementation of new practices, new structures, or new ways of working.

- To be open to the research process by contributing ideas, responding to research instruments, opening up our classrooms for observation, offering our professional support in what ever way required.

- To engage in workshop activity within full staff meetings, staff days or other school meetings in order to contribute to the ongoing knowledge creation and learning process.

CHAPTER 10

Whole-School Strategies

The case studies in this chapter are intended to provide examples of actual 'whole-school' settings, where the approaches to learning, teaching and assessment described in the previous chapters are taking place. In these schools all improvement and development efforts are focused on learning and teaching. The conditions are being created in these schools where teachers have time to talk to each other about teaching and to work together towards improving it, and where a capacity for development has been self-consciously created.

These are schools where the 'quick fix' response to target-setting has been eschewed in favour of a more reflective and iterative approach to change that focuses on the learning of students. These schools are becoming more effective over time because they are progressively adapting their organisation and classroom practices to support teacher development and student learning.

As we look across these four case studies we see that these schools are increasingly:

- taking student learning outcomes as their developmental focus;
- focusing on medium-term and strategic planning;
- becoming more skilful in managing staff development and school improvement;
- adopting specifications of curriculum and teaching that extend their current practice and that focus directly on the student learning goals that have been set;
- managing the change process by using a combination of pressure and support;
- monitoring progress and gathering appropriate research data on student learning;
- modifying their culture and developing a 'capacity for change'.

Rushden is a secondary school in Northamptonshire. This case study describes the approach taken in the school to improving teacher effectiveness as a whole-school development priority.

The strategy was introduced against a background of extensive lesson observation carried out over a period of two years by external inspectors and senior staff. A number of teachers felt that these events confirmed their own fears that their teaching was less than satisfactory, but observation alone failed to help them understand how to improve. Sensitivity to this situation, and providing support to overcome feelings of helplessness, were significant considerations in designing the school improvement strategy.

The process of the scheme is summarised in the diagram.

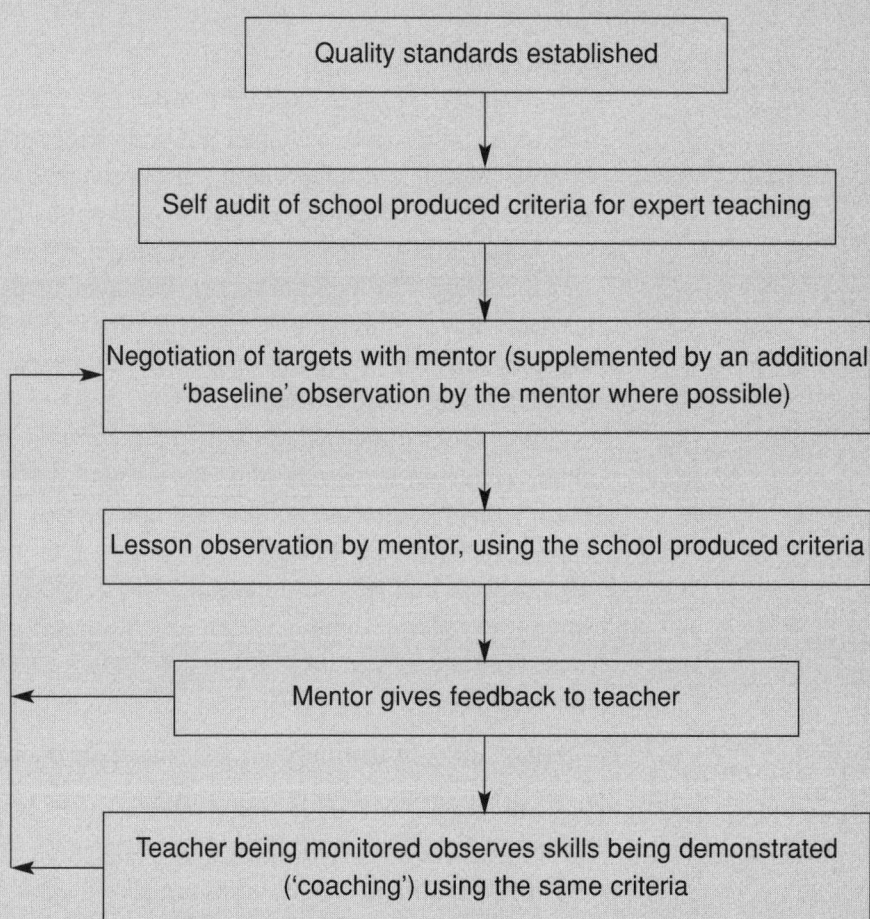

```
            ┌─────────────────────────────────────────┐
            │       Quality standards established       │
            └─────────────────────────────────────────┘
                              │
                              ▼
        ┌─────────────────────────────────────────────────┐
        │  Self audit of school produced criteria for       │
        │              expert teaching                      │
        └─────────────────────────────────────────────────┘
                              │
                              ▼
     ┌────────────────────────────────────────────────────────┐
  ┌─▶│ Negotiation of targets with mentor (supplemented by an   │
  │  │ additional 'baseline' observation by the mentor where    │
  │  │ possible)                                                │
  │  └────────────────────────────────────────────────────────┘
  │                           │
  │                           ▼
  │  ┌────────────────────────────────────────────────────────┐
  │  │ Lesson observation by mentor, using the school produced  │
  │  │ criteria                                                 │
  │  └────────────────────────────────────────────────────────┘
  │                           │
  │                           ▼
  │     ┌──────────────────────────────────────────────┐
  │◀────│      Mentor gives feedback to teacher          │
  │     └──────────────────────────────────────────────┘
  │                           │
  │                           ▼
  │  ┌────────────────────────────────────────────────────────┐
  │◀─│ Teacher being monitored observes skills being            │
  │  │ demonstrated ('coaching') using the same criteria        │
  │  └────────────────────────────────────────────────────────┘
```

Quality standards for effective teaching

Each teacher assessed his or her present level of skills and compared it with the desired outcome. A whole-school view was developed of 'an ideal classroom' in terms of teacher behaviour. Ten quality standard statements were produced through meetings and consultations involving every teacher. This consultation was broadly based, partly to generate ownership and partly to raise awareness of best practice.

Self audit

A small group produced a lengthy questionnaire containing descriptions of teaching skills broken down into small components to help experienced teachers, who use wide repetoires of skill routines intuitively, become more aware of their behaviour. Each teacher answered this questionnaire and, after discussion during a 'critical friend' exercise, decided on areas for potential improvement. Teachers saw the questionnaire as a valid interpretation of the quality standards and liked the breakdown of skills because it helped to depersonalise the process through comparing their performance with an ideal. It was also useful for promoting reflection and for identifying strengths as well as weaknesses. Some teachers felt that the questionnaire had not helped them to focus on specific targets. It was felt that while the approach of breaking skills down into small steps was useful, more account needed to be taken of the holistic nature of teaching and it was agreed that a revised form of self audit instrument would provide better support for mentors and teachers. The whole mentor group then helped to produce a new self audit and to identify the behaviours which an 'expert teacher' with strengths in a particular area would use to teach a lesson.

Mentoring and negotiated targets

The mentor, at the self audit stage, helped the teacher to focus on the three skill areas most in need of skill development and to establish priorities, checking that the skills chosen were likely to lead to a significant improvement in performance. In this, the skills of the mentor were often important. The teacher and mentor then agreed on three improvement targets. (It is useful if the mentor can first observe a lesson, rather than relying on discussion of a self audit exercise). The targets must be 'SMART' – specific, measurable, achievable, realistic and timed. The discipline of forming a SMART target is helpful in clarifying exactly what the teacher needs to do, and experiencing success, even in a small way, gives confidence to continue to try to change.

The mentor helped the teacher select new strategies and tactics in the classroom. Some mentors were better than others in offering suggestions for new approaches. The lists of behaviours which an 'expert' would use (developed from the revised self audit questionnaire) were designed to help overcome this problem. In some ways, they are like 'tips for teachers' in that they can be used to generate ideas for new approaches.

Feedback on progress

A key task for the mentor was to check the progress the teacher made towards achieving his or her targets. The mentor observed the lesson and provided feedback to the teacher with any necessary suggestions for new strategies and tactics. A pro forma of lists of 'expert behaviour' was used to provide criteria for lesson observation to enable the mentor to give really useful feedback. To provide momentum to the teacher's attempt to change it is important that the mentor has the time to observe lessons and give feedback frequently. Once a teacher has achieved each of three targets, a new one is set. (If observation of a lesson for the first time shows that the target is not appropriate an alternative is suggested.)

Mentors also helped teachers to identify strategies and tactics by providing coaching. If appropriate, the teacher will observe the mentor demonstrating a particular skill (in a lesson) and then discuss the strategies and tactics used. It is often possible for a teacher to observe small parts of lessons because the focus of the target is precise. This helps to make coaching practicable.

Since the project was a whole-school development priority, it was necessary to ensure that mentors used a consistent approach. Watching colleagues teach and commenting on performance is a potentially challenging experience for both mentor and teacher. By using a common process and standard materials, negative personal feelings have been minimised.

The Rushden School improvement project produced a number of benefits:

• On readministering the questionnaire, almost all scored themselves more positively than at the beginning of the project.

• The mentor group experienced valuable professional development as a result of designing resources and meeting regularly as a group, as well as from the formal training sessions.

• Most importantly, the project focused the work of the school on pedagogy, the key focus for school improvement.

*Case Study 2
Swanwick Hall
School –
Ruth Watts*

Swanwick Hall School is an 11–18 comprehensive school in eastern Derbyshire with a fully comprehensive intake. The school joined the East Midlands IQEA partnership in 1996 because many of the 'school improvement measures' used in school prior to that time were not classroom based. The emphasis on teaching and learning since has meant:

- A better deal for students in terms of interest and variety, which caters for a greater range of learning styles.

- That most staff development time has been concentrated on teaching and learning which pleased virtually all staff.

- The impetus for change belongs to a volunteer group of staff ranging across departments and experience (it currently includes the head teacher and several NQTs) working collaboratively with the heads of faculty group. This means that the staff do not feel driven by senior management or external pressures as much as they did previously.

After extensive discussion, the IQEA group decided that all staff should concentrate on the model of inductive teaching for the first year of development. The main reasons for this decision were:

- The model is applicable to all subjects.

- No one understood it previously, so all staff were learning together and sharing ideas across departments.

- The different phases cater for different styles of teaching, including individual and group work, so there is variety in the lessons.

- The six phases make it quite a complex model which requires understanding, so the staff had something to talk about. Comments were heard like 'Phases 1 to 4 are fine but then I struggle with phases 5 and 6. Any ideas?'

- The latter phases involve higher order thinking skills, which were underdeveloped in school.

- Though the data for inductive teaching often involves considerable time planning, it can be used from year to year once it exists. This has meant that building the teaching model into Schemes of Work has not been too difficult.

Once the volunteer group had practised the model and videoed themselves, they were ready to organise a whole-school in-service day to learn about the model and then prepare work for inductive teaching in departments. Volunteer staff, who had never done any INSET work before, talked to the staff attending the INSET session.

During the next 12 months a variety of ways were found to share ideas on inductive teaching:

- More half INSET days to report back on progress and develop more data sets for new lessons.

- Lots of co-planning and co-teaching while the volunteer IQEA group covered colleagues' lessons.

- Sharing ideas via videos.

- After every staff development session, each department completed a questionnaire for the IQEA group who published a 'State of Inductive Teaching' report for staff.

- Lists were produced of topics taught inductively, with lists of the year groups involved. These ranged from Year 7 to Year 13, with no obvious bias to any particular key stage.

- Heads of faculty meetings were used as ways of sharing ideas and problems, e.g. how to include reluctant staff, building the model into Schemes of Work.

- Students were questioned about their perceptions and the results were published.

- Exactly 12 months later a new in-service day began by having a curriculum tour, i.e. all departments put on a 20 minute workshop on topics they had taught inductively. This proved to be a highly successful staff development session.

The IQEA group accepted some flexibility during the year. The Languages department for example decided that many Key Stage 3 students needed a greater vocabulary in order for inductive teaching to work. So they made a decision to start with mnemonics, prior to moving into inductive teaching. This worked very well for them. One or two departments were slower to start than others, but, on the whole, it was felt that inductive teaching was an ideal way to start school improvement work at Swanwick Hall. However other schools in our IQEA partnership chose other routes which were just as appropriate for them.

The pattern for the second year of IQEA was very similar to the first. Cooperative group work and mnemonics were chosen in year 2, but we felt that it was still important to check that inductive teaching was well embedded into their Schemes of Work. Virtually all departments engaged in cooperative group work, especially pairs/fours, jigsaw techniques and numbered heads. Students became used to sitting where the teacher decided, so it was easier to organise group work than it had been previously. Some very committed staff moved students around so often that invariably they now ask 'Where do you want us to sit today?' as they enter the room. Teachers worked hard to establish cooperative learning standards, with an ethos of acceptance of all contributions. This has been quite successful but there is a realisation that it will be hard work to maintain it.

Mnemonics was the other new strategy for year 2. As a model, it is much quicker to learn than inductive teaching and cooperative group work, but it suits staff with creative minds more than those who struggle to devise interesting mnemonics. It has been used extensively in Languages and Science, with several other departments trying it. Sometimes the students are much better than the staff at producing excellent mnemonics.

The third year of IQEA has been more open-ended. More departments feel self-confident in developing their own variety of teaching and learning strategies. Several departments are using synectics, and concept attainment has worked well in 'content heavy' courses. The Maths department has improved its approach to investigations in maths. The Languages department is heavily involved in preferred learning styles with techniques for ensuring there is more kinaesthetic as well as audio and visual learning. Some of the scientists are using accelerated learning techniques. Monitoring progress and sharing ideas has been harder but only because the impetus for development comes from departments and individual teachers rather than from the top.

Next year the school intends to:

- Develop the use of some of our newer models across more staff.
- Link our work on behaviour for learning more specifically with the IQEA initiative.
- Use the cooperative learning standards and some of the ideas from accelerated learning for this.
- Collect more data from staff and students about progress and perceptions.

*Case Study 3
Big Wood
School,
Nottingham –
Colette
Singleton*

Situated on the northern boundary of the city, Big Wood School serves an area described as 'one of serious social need'. Eight years ago Big Wood faced possible closure. Demographic trends, coupled with a poor image in the community, meant that the school had been steadily losing students and staff for several years.

With the arrival of a new head teacher interviews with staff, questionnaires to students/parents/local community, and meetings with feeder school staff were undertaken and produced a picture of a school that was seen as caring but which lacked rigour. Three clear aims were quickly established:

• To improve the school's image in the community.

• To develop the links with the feeder schools.

• To tackle the under-achievement culture.

The threat of possible closure, replaced after the first 12 months with the 'threat' of an OFSTED inspection, proved to be a powerful factor in focusing people's minds. A new staffing structure, clear policies, a new uniform, a well-structured Code of Conduct, and mentoring programmes, all began to have positive effects. Student numbers began to rise, examination results improved and the 'what-can-you-expect of . . .' culture was being successfully challenged. The OFSTED report was, in the main, positive, but the quality of teaching and learning emerged as a major issue.

A start had been made. The school had begun to develop the capacity to accept change. However, the initiatives outlined above were, in many ways, only peripheral. It was recognised that for lasting improvement the school needed to bring about more sustainable change focused on the classroom.

At the critical moment the school became involved in the IQEA project. The overall aim of the project is to strengthen schools' abilities to provide quality education for all students by building on good practice. The project's emphasis on teaching and learning at the heart of sustained improvement was felt to be in total accord with where Big Wood was in its particular stage of development.

This approach to school improvement called for, among other things, the establishment of a group, known as the cadre, to act as the initial change agents. The first cadre group consisted of the head teacher and seven volunteers – a deputy head teacher, two heads of department and four MPG teachers. Interestingly, and purely by chance, all areas of the curriculum except one were represented.

Fortunately at this time, several members of the cadre attended a summer school on models of teaching run by the University of Nottingham and soon realised that the inductive model offered a possible way to address the issues facing the school. This was partially because it was a new approach, and therefore offered exciting possibilities, and because it was applicable across the whole curriculum it seemed an ideal place to start.

For the cadre group the first stage was to learn more about the model, to practise it and to observe each other. Lessons were then videoed and, when the group felt ready, a day's INSET session was prepared for the whole staff. The model was explored inductively, videos shown and opportunities created for staff to begin to practise using the model in a safe environment, i.e. with other groups of staff.

In order to encourage other people to adopt this approach staff were clustered into small groups, with a member of the cadre attached to each group to provide support and guidance. Opportunities were created for people to observe each other and some notable successes were recorded, when, for example, a member of staff, known more for his competence than his charisma, found himself surrounded by a group of eager students at the end of an inductive lesson wanting to continue with their work. As well as working with their support groups, staff also worked within their departments, reviewing Schemes of Work to see where the inductive approach might be used to greatest effect and planning lessons accordingly.

By the end of the first year and in the light of experience the whole process was reviewed and several clear 'messages' emerged.

- Time was an issue:
  - the importance of creating a regular time for the cadre group to meet
  - time for staff to learn new models, to prepare new materials, to observe each other and visit other schools to observe good practice
  - interviews/questionnaires all required time.
- The power of the student voice. A 14-year-old student's calm statement on video that, 'copying is a waste of time because the words go from the board, down your pen, and onto the paper, without going anywhere near your brain', is a more arresting message than any amount of exhortation and analysis from the head teacher on ineffective methodologies.
- In the same way, showing in-house videos and persuading staff, not normally seen as the most inventive of teachers, to demonstrate effective approaches, had a powerful impact, especially on the dissenting few.
- The value of residentials and other twilight sessions in helping to develop a real group ethos among the members of the cadre.
- The difficulty of maintaining momentum. It was not always easy to find regular development time.

In the second year a more structured model was developed. Creating more time required a radical rethinking of the way time was used in the school. The problem was resolved in the following ways:

- The current meeting structure was reviewed, and staff meetings, for example, were replaced by staff development time, and alternative methods were used to disseminate information. All remaining meetings, such as departmental meetings, were to devote 50 per cent of the time to development issues relating to teaching and learning.
- Staff were encouraged to 'bank' some non-contact time by covering other colleagues. This time was then pooled so that all staff, either as individuals or departments, were given half-day slots for development.

- Members of the senior management team were to provide a percentage of the cover time each fortnight, which could be booked by staff.

- Adults other than teachers were to be used to supervise exams and thus free departments.

The careful positioning of INSET, twilight and staff development meant that staff were now meeting approximately every four weeks to look at development issues focused on teaching and learning. It was also agreed, following consultation with the staff, to broaden the range of activities.

It was during the second year that the real benefits of this approach to school improvement became apparent. Working in pairs and triads, the cadre used the expertise of the University and LEA staff, as well as their own reading and research, to develop their expertise in areas as diverse as the major components of a well-structured lesson, cooperative group work, whole-class teaching, formative assessment, creating the learning classroom. The aim was to encourage staff to develop at their own pace, while providing the necessary expertise and support within a climate that encouraged risk taking.

As the school was preparing to enter its third year of the IQEA project the inevitable brown envelope arrived and, while not totally subsuming everything else, it would be fair to say that the prospect of an imminent OFSTED inspection led to a period of consolidation rather than breaking new ground.

The inspection results were better than could have been hoped for. In a term with four NQTs having had very little time to settle and when two members of staff were off with long-term illness and being covered by supply staff, OFSTED deemed that, 'Teaching is a strength of the school'. Concerning lessons, 97 per cent were judged satisfactory or better, 64 per cent were good or better, and 28 per cent were very good or excellent. This was in sharp contrast with the picture four years earlier when only 75 per cent of lessons were judged satisfactory and less than 30 per cent were good or better.

Compared with three years ago, the school is now moving forward from a position where:

- Teaching and learning is now acknowledged by all as fundamental and is at the heart of the development agenda.

- Classrooms are more open and people more willing to observe and be observed.

- Staff are developing a language to talk about teaching and learning.

- People feel part of the development process. They are involved in making it happen, not just the unwilling recipients.

As the OFSTED report said:

The school is successfully challenging the non-achievement culture, noted in the previous OFSTED Report, through its major focus on raising the quality of teaching. This is having a major impact on students' attainment and progress.

Case Study 4
The Sharnbrook
School
Improvement
Journey –
David Jackson

Sharnbrook Upper School and Community College was established as a 13–19 upper school in 1975 to provide comprehensive education for 32 villages situated in rural mid-England. Sharnbrook's school improvement model is now a continuous, whole-school initiative deeply embedded into the daily work of the school. At its heart is a fluid group (cadre) of staff committed to working in partnerships, and together, around areas of mutually agreed enquiry. During the eight years of involvement with IQEA the school has had almost as many different modes of operation but certain characteristics remain consistent:

- The school improvement group is led by two staff operating in a co-leadership mode.

- The school improvement group breaks down into trios of staff, each engaged in a separate enquiry designed to generate knowledge and understanding about the school's work and to indicate directions for improvement.

- Each staff partnership undertakes a sustained process of enquiry within the school, drawing also from the knowledge-base within the field and from good practice elsewhere, and, as an outcome of this data-gathering, suggests improvement to the school's practice, supports the implementation of improvements and then carries out further enquiries into the effect upon student learning or the wider school community.

- Each partnership tries to ensure that all those who contribute towards their research are also involved in the process of making meaning from the data and, where feasible, in the implementation of outcomes.

- Each partnership also commits to connect with the wider constituency of staff, students, parents and governors in order that all who need to do so can share the emergent journey.

- The school facilitates opportunities for each partnership to lock into consultation and decision-making structures, as appropriate, so that findings from the enquiry will be implemented.

- The entire school improvement group commits to monitoring the value of their own work and to critique each other's practice.

Staff at all levels of the school are involved, including newly qualified teachers and support staff, and, more recently, students. Each partnership is entirely free of status positions within the more formal organisational structure of the school and offers leadership opportunities to a variety of staff. Some partnerships might be involved with significant whole-school issues (for example, assessment strategies to improve student achievement), while others may be engaged in focused classroom research activity (questioning technique, or cooperative group work). The scale of the intended impact is less significant than the quality of the knowledge deriving from the enquiry. A piece of classroom research, for example, can have equally powerful whole-school impact if the knowledge (about seating arrangements, starts and finishes of lessons – or whatever) is sufficiently significant and widely owned.

Sharnbrook IQEA 1999–2000

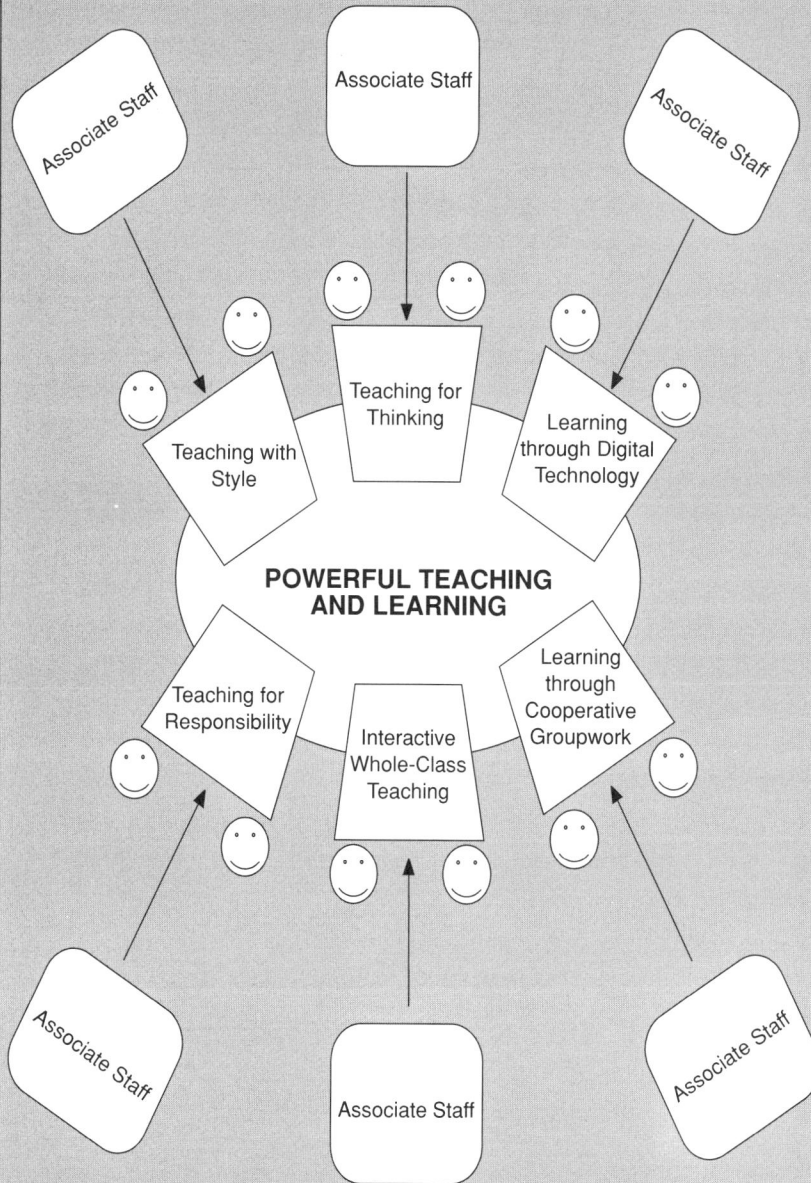

Associate Staff

Associate Staff

Associate Staff

Teaching for Thinking

Teaching with Style

Learning through Digital Technology

POWERFUL TEACHING AND LEARNING

Teaching for Responsibility

Interactive Whole-Class Teaching

Learning through Cooperative Groupwork

Associate Staff

Associate Staff

Associate Staff

Three Phases

Phase One
- Theoretical Understanding
- Powerful Professional Development
- In-class coaching
- Involvement of Associate Group

Phase Two
- Generation of action research design
- Involvement of students
- Generation of empirical data
- Experimentation amongst Associate Group
- Coaching by Partnership members

Phase Three
- Partnership members as
  - Consultants
  - Professional Development
  - Providers
  - Coaches in classroom

By 1997 the school had incorporated into their model a group of students who were empowered to operate their own 'school improvement group' complementing and mirroring the style of the wider group. As the student voice dimension of the work evolved, teachers wanted more authentic and active involvement than just a 'passive voice'. At this stage between a third and a half of the staff were involved for any one year, focusing exclusively on enquiry and improvement issues.

The 1999/2000 model shown in the diagram retains the concept of trios, but reverts to a focus which is specifically upon teaching and learning. Following a workshop with the whole staff, six areas of classroom practice were identified, and each of the trios adopted one of the areas mandated by the whole staff. The first 'enquiry' task for each of the partnerships is to develop a powerful theoretical understanding of their particular teaching and learning focus – by researching the knowledge-base, observing class-rooms, visiting other schools, or whatever. The trio will then practise and develop their skills in the classroom and provide in-house coaching for one another. The next phase will be to engage in action research with students to seek to validate the impact of this approach upon learning. Throughout this process the remainder of the staff (all staff not involved in one of the partnerships) will choose one of the areas, creating associate groups of about 15 staff for each partnership, who will follow the course of events, engage in workshops and generally become immersed and prepared. When (or if) the action research process validates the impact of the model, the associate staff will be asked to adopt the approach in their own class-rooms and to be coached by the trio engaged in the original work.

This is a huge over-simplification of the model, even so it gives indications of the infrastructural and cultural changes that have evolved through the work of the various models. These would include:

- The opening up of classrooms and classroom practice and the legitimisation of in-class coaching.
- The creation of a language to talk about teaching and school improvement.
- The integration of enquiry and professional development approaches.
- The value and authenticity of the student voice and the significance given to their perceptions as learners.
- The willingness of all staff to embrace the value of the development work emanating from the school improvement group.
- The ownership by the whole staff of the school improvement approach.
- The power of a sustained school improvement journey to win over those initially sceptical or even cynical.
- The expansion of leadership capacity.

Coda

These case studies demonstrate clearly that schools that are committed to school improvement use staff development to unite the twin foci of teaching and learning and capacity building. In highly effective schools it is this that provides the essential infrastructure for school improvement. In *The New Structure of School Improvement* (Joyce *et al.* 1999) we articulated a set of hypotheses that characterise the 'evolutionary school', one that has enquiry as its main focus. These ideas resonate with the case studies in this chapter. In concluding this chapter and reflecting on the case studies, it may be helpful to summarise these hypotheses particularly in so far as they provide a structure for staff development that has student achievement as its core (adapted from Joyce *et al.* 1999, Chapter 1):

Hypothesis 1: Staff development has to be built into the weekly routine of teachers, into new practices and into the implementation of school improvement initiatives. Staff development has to be a regular event.

Hypothesis 2: Adjusting the timetable to allow teachers time for collective inquiry will create the structural conditions in which the process of school improvement is nested.

Hypothesis 3: An information-rich environment will enhance inquiry. Studying classroom practice will expand inquiry into ways of helping students to learn better.

Hypothesis 4: Connecting teachers to the knowledge base on teaching and learning will lead to the development of successful initiatives for school improvement.

Hypothesis 5: Staff development, structured as an inquiry, both fuels energy and results in initiatives that have greater effects. The content of staff development – curriculum and teaching – is organised so that, as new practices are implemented, their effects are studied systematically.

Hypothesis 6: A teaching staff that is organised into peer coaching teams of two to four members has greater knowledge of what each other are doing with the children and support one another in solving problems and expanding their repertoire of teaching and learning strategies.

Each of these six hypotheses defines a strategy for creating an infrastructure for staff development appropriate for sustained school improvement. Combined they create the conditions for enhanced teaching and learning.

References and Further Reading

Ainscow, M. *et al.* (1994) *Creating the Conditions for School Improvement.* London: David Fulton Publishers.

Brophy, J. and Good, T. (1986) 'Teacher behaviour and student achievement', in Wittrock, M. (ed.) *Handbook of Research on Teaching,* 3rd edn. New York: Macmillan.

Creemers, B. (1994) *The Effective Classroom.* London: Cassell.

DfEE (April 1998) *Induction for New Teachers,* Consultation Document. London: DfEE.

DfEE (May 1998) *Teaching: High Status, High Standards,* Circular 4/98. London: DfEE.

Downey, L. (1967) *The Secondary Phase of Education.* Boston: Ginn and Co.

Doyle, W. (1987) 'Research on teaching effects as a resource for improving instruction', in Wideen, M. and Andrews, I. (eds) *Staff Development for School Improvement.* Lewes: Falmer Press.

Evertson, C. and Harris, A. (1992) 'What We Know About Managing Classrooms', *Educational Leadership*, April, 74–78.

Fullan, M. (1991) *The New Meaning of Educational Change.* London: Cassell.

Good, T. (1989) 'Using Classroom and School Research to Professionalize Teaching', Keynote presentation at the International Congress for School Effectiveness and Improvement, Rotterdam, Netherlands, 5th January 1989.

Good, T. and Brophy, J. (1994) *Looking in Classrooms (6th edition).* New York: Harper-Collins.

Gray, J. (1990) 'The quality of schooling: frameworks for judgement', *British Journal of Educational Studies* **38**(3), 203–23.

Gray, J. *et al.* (1999) *Improving Schools.* Buckingham: Open University Press.

Hargreaves, A. (2000) 'The emotional geography of teaching'. Paper presented at School of Education, University of Nottingham, May 2000.

Harris, A. (1995) 'Effective teaching', *School Improvement Network Bulletin.* London: Institute of Education.

Harris, A. (1998) 'A review of the literature on effective teaching', *School Leadership and Management* **18**(2), 169–85.

Harris, A. (1999) *Teaching and Learning in the Effective School.* London: Arena Press.

Hopkins, D. (1997) *Powerful Learning, Powerful Teaching and Powerful Schools – an Inaugural Lecture*. Nottingham: Centre for Teacher and School Development, University of Nottingham.

Hopkins, D. (in press) *Beyond School Improvement – Valuing Educational Reform*. London: Falmer Press.

Hopkins, D. and Stern, D. (1996) 'Quality teachers, quality schools', *Teaching and Teacher Education* **12**(5), Winter, 501–17.

Hopkins, D. *et al.* (1994) *School Improvement in an Era of Change*. London: Cassell.

Hopkins, D. *et al.* (1997) *Creating the Conditions for Classroom Improvement*. London: David Fulton Publishers.

Johnson, D.W. and Johnson, R.T. (1993) *Circles of Learning*. Englewood Cliffs, N.J.: Prentice Hall.

Joyce, B. (1992) 'Co-operative learning and staff development: teaching the method with the method', *Co-operative Learning* **12**(2), 10–13.

Joyce, B. and Calhoun, E. (1998) *Learning to Teach Inductively*. Boston: Allyn and Bacon.

Joyce, B. and Showers, B. (1980a) 'Improving in-service training: the messages of research', *Educational Leadership* **37**(5), 379–85.

Joyce, B. and Showers, B. (1980b) 'The coaching of teaching', *Educational Leadership* **40**(2), 4–10.

Joyce, B. and Showers, B. (1988) *Student Achievement through Staff Development*. New York: Longman.

Joyce, B. and Showers, B. (1991) *Information Processing Models of Teaching*. Aptos, California: Booksend Laboratories.

Joyce, B. and Showers, B. (1995) *Student Achievement Through Staff Development*. White Plains, N.Y.: Longman.

Joyce, B. and Weil, M. (1996) *Models of Teaching,* 5th edn. Englewood Cliffs, NJ: Prentice-Hall.

Joyce, B. *et al.* (1997) *Models of Learning – Tools for Teaching*. Buckingham: Open University Press.

Joyce, B. *et al.* (1999) *The New Structure of School Improvement*. Buckingham: Open University Press.

Kounin, J. S. (1970) *Discipline and Group Management in Classrooms*. New York: Holt, Rinehart and Winston.

Kyriacou, C. (1986) *Effective Teaching in Schools*. Oxford: Basil Blackwell.

Kyriacou, C. (1991) *Essential Teaching Skills*. Oxford: Basil Blackwell.

Reynolds, D. (1988) *Numeracy Matters* (Preliminary Report of the Numeracy Task Force). London: DfEE.

Rubin, L. (1985) *Artistry and Teaching*. New York: Random House.

Ruddock, J. (1984) 'Introducing Innovations to Pupils', in Hopkins, D. and Wideen, M. (eds) *Alternative Perspectives on School Improvement*. Lewes: Falmer Press.

Rutter, M. *et al.* (1979) *Fifteen Thousand Hours*. London: Open Books.

Slavin, R. (1994) *Using Student Team Learning*. Baltimore, Maryland: Center for Social Organization of Schools, John Hopkins University.

Stenhouse, L. (1975) *An Introduction to Curriculum Research and Development*. London: Heinemann Books.

Walberg, H. (1990) 'Productive teaching and instruction: assessing the knowledge base', *Phi Delta Kappa* **71**(6), 470–9.

Wang, M. C. *et al.* (1993) 'Toward a knowledge base for school learning', *Review of Educational Research* **63**(3), 249–94.

Index

accountability, individual 29
activities, learning 20–1
Ainscow, M. 1
analogies 50, 51, 52, 53, 55
application 79
artistry of teaching 8
assessment 9, 10, 67–75
    staff development activity 71–75
awareness 78

Big Wood School 92–4
Brophy, J. 6, 15–16

cadre group 81–83, 89–90, 92–3, 94, 95–6
Calhoun, E. 4, 10, 38, 52, 61, 81, 98
categorisation 36–7, 39–41, 45–7
classroom level conditions 2–3
classroom management 7–8, 16, 52
coaching, peer 81
cognitive abilities 28
commitment 84
community, school 84
compressed conflict 51, 52, 53, 55
concept attainment 10, 59–65
    description of model 60–1
    elaboration of model 62
    phases 61
    staff development activity 63–4
concepts 78
cooperative group work 10, 25–33, 90
    description of model 26–9
    principles 29
    stages of model 29–30
    using techniques of 31–3
creativity 50–52
Creemers, G. 15
criteria-referenced assessment 70
critical friends 28
curriculum, process model of 9–10

data sets 36, 38–9, 45

deep learning 67
demonstration 18–19
design 20–1
development capacity 2
diagnosis 69
direct analogy 51, 52, 53, 55
discussions 19–20
diversity of method 70
Downey, L. 10
Doyle, W. 7

engagement of pupils 20–1
envoys 27–8
evaluative feedback 70
Evertson, C. 7
evolutionary school 98
examples (exemplars) 60–1, 62, 64–5
explaining 16

face-to-face interaction 29
feedback 70, 88
formative assessment 10, 67–75
    principles of 69–71
frameworks for teaching and learning 5–11
Fullan, M. 77

goals 69
Good, T. 6, 15–16
ground rules 28
group work *see* cooperative group work

Hargreaves, A. 8
Harris, A. 7
Hopkins, D. 4, 10, 27, 52, 61, 81, 98
Humanities Curriculum Project (HCP) 9–10

implementation 21
Improving the Quality of Education for All (IQEA)
    project 77, 89–91, 92–4, 95–7
    school improvement approach 1–3, 82–3
inductive teaching 10, 35–47, 89–91, 92–3
    description of model 36–7
    elaboration of model 38–43
    phases 38
    staff development activity 44–7
interdependence, positive 29

jigsaw technique 26, 27
Johnson, D.W. 29
Johnson, R.T. 29
Joyce, B. 4, 10, 38, 52, 61, 98
    training 77–81

knowledge, organised 78
Kounin, J.S. 7–8

learning 4
    activities/tasks 20–1
    evolutionary model of teacher learning 78–80
    frameworks for 5–11
    how assessment can help 67
    superficial and deep 67

102

lecture/talk 18
listening triads 28

memorising information 10
    see also concept attainment
mentoring 87–8
meta-cognition 6
mnemonics 90
models of teaching 3, 4, 9–11
    see also concept attainment; cooperative group work;
        inductive teaching; synectics; whole-class teaching

negotiated targets 87
numbered heads technique 25, 26–7

OFSTED 94
opportunity to learn 6–7
organised knowledge 78

partnerships, staff 95–7
peer coaching 81
personal analogy 51, 52, 53, 54
positive interdependence 29
powerful learning 4, 5–6
presentation 16
    information 18–19, 60–71, 62
principles 78–9
problem-solving 79
process model of curriculum 9–10
processing 29

quality standards 86
questioning 19–20
    use of 22–4

rainbow groups 27
Rubin, L. 8
Rudduck, J. 9
Rushden School 86–8

school community 83
school improvement 1–3, 77, 81–3
    cadre group 81–83, 89–90, 92–3, 94, 96–7
school level conditions 2–3
Schools Council 9
self audit 87
self-reflection 70
sequencing 16
shared criteria 70
Sharnbrook School 96–7
Showers, B. 4, 77–81
skills 78–9
    social 29
    teaching 6–8, 9
snowballing 27
social skills 29
staff development 77–83
    evolutionary school 99
    IQEA school improvement 77, 81–3
    Joyce and Showers approach 77–81
    peer coaching 81
    see also whole-school strategies

standards, quality 86
Stenhouse, L. 9, 10, 11
strategies 15–16
structuring 7
    whole-class teaching 15, 16
Student Teams Achievement Divisions (STAD) strategy 29–30
students
    engaging in learning tasks/activities 20–1
    involving in discussions 19–20
    voice of 92
superficial learning 67
Swanwick Hall School 89–91
synectics 10, 49–55
    description of model 50–2
    elaboration of model 53
    phases 52
    staff development activity 54–7

talk/lecture 18
targets, negotiated 87
tasks, learning 20–1
teacher instruction 29–30
teacher learning, evolutionary model of 78–81
teaching
    behaviours 6–8, 15
    effective 4
    frameworks for 5–11
    models of *see* models of teaching
    relationships 8
    skills 6–8, 9
team recognition 30
team study 30
testing
    concept attainment 61, 62
    cooperative group work 30
thinking strategies 61, 62
time 93–4
training matrix 80
    see also staff development
triads, listening 28
trios of staff 95–6
twos to fours 27

understanding 15, 61, 62

Weil, M. 4
whole-class teaching 10, 13–24
    components of model 17–21
    description of model 14–16
    phases 17
    use of questioning 22–4
whole-school strategies 84–98
    Big Wood School 92–5
    Rushden School 86–8
    Sharnbrook School 96–7
    Swanwick Hall School 89–91
work involvement 7–8
workplace 78
workshop 78